HISTORY OF CASTE IN INDIA

HISTORY OF CASTE IN INDIA

(Evidence of the Laws of Manu on the Social Conditions in India during the Third Century A. D. Interpreted and Examined)

With an Appendix on
Radical Defects of Ethnology

S. V. KETKAR, A. M. (Cornell)

GYAN

Published by

Gyan Publishing House
5, Ansari Road
Daryaganj, New Delhi-110002
Phone: 011-47034999, 9811692060
E-mail: books@gyanbooks.com

Distribution Network
gyanbooks.com
India, USA, Canada, UK, Australia, France

ISBN : 978-81-212-6026-8 (PB)
First Published, 1909

2nd Impression 2021

Printed at: Gyan Press, Delhi.

History of Caste in India
Author: S. V. Ketkar

HISTORY OF CASTE IN INDIA

(Evidence of the Laws of Manu on the Social Conditions in India during the Third Century A.D. Interpreted and Examined)

With an Appendix on
Radical Defects of Ethnology

S. V. Ketkar, A. M. (Cornell)

1979

PREFACE.

I have said regarding the scope of the book in the introductory chapter and here I make only such remarks, which I could not include in the book itself.

The second and seventh chapters of this book were reported to the general seminary of the Department of History and Political Science at Cornell University during the year 1907–8. I am indebted to the professors and students for their valuable criticisms made on the occasion. The second chapter formed part of the dissertation which was submitted as a partial fulfillment of the requirements of master's degree. The radical defects of ethnology which I have discussed in the appendix have appeared already in the quarterly American Anthropologist, Vol. XI.

During the compilation of the book, I had availed myself of the material in the Boston Public Library and the libraries at Cornell, Columbia, Yale, and Harvard. I found the library of Harvard best suited for my work; the oriental collection there, is undoubtedly the best in the country. Professor Lanman at Harvard had allowed me the privilege of using his own excellent and extensive collection.

In the preparation of the index besides those of a general reader, the special needs of the students of society, antiquity, Sanskrit literature and Indian history have been considered and I hope the index would be of some service to them.

While adapting the Roman alphabet to represent Indian words, I have distinguished long vowels by a maeron, italised, *t*, *d*, *n* to represent the non-dental sounds and *re* to represent the peculiar Sanskrit vowel. The letters j n denotes the peculiar pelatal compound of frequent occurrence in Sanskrit words. I have avoided all other niceties. In the case of some words which have already become English I have given the current English spelling.

My sincere thanks are due to Professor Lanman of Harvard and Professor Hopkins of Yale, for their perusal of the manuscript and for some very valuable suggestions. I should also thank Messrs. J. B. Lyon & Co. for their careful typography, and Mr. Henry C. Hasbrouck of Troy; N. Y., for going over the proofs.

September '09.

CONTENTS.

CHAPTER I.

INTRODUCTORY.

CHAPTER II.

THE CASTE SYSTEM.

1. *Definition of Caste.*

CHAPTER III

HISTORY OF INDIA, 250 B. C.–250 A. D.

CHAPTER IV.

THE BOOK MĀNAVA-DHARMA-SHĀSTRA.

CHAPTER V.

Treatment of Caste by the Book.

1. *Meaning of Words.*

4. *Occupational Castes.*

5. *Possibility of Changing One's Caste.*

CHAPTER VI.

PHILOSOPHY OF CASTE (VARNA ORDER.)

1. *The Philosophical Theories.*

2. *Theory of Purity.*

CHAPTER VIII.

DISCRIMINATION ON ACCOUNT OF VARNA.

1. *Materials for Investigation.*

5. *Varna and Marriage.*

6. *Varna and Illicit Intercourse.*

7. Varna and the Criminal Law. Page.

8. Brāhmana and Shūdra.

APPENDIX

HISTORY OF CASTE.

CHAPTER I.

INTRODUCTORY.

The Problem.—The mystery of caste is a hard problem for a foreigner to understand. I doubt whether a man who has not stayed a long time in India would be able to understand this problem even if he reads my book. Even the man who stays in India for a long time does not understand what caste is. He thinks that this strange people who are called Hindus must have some very peculiar constitution of mind which a stranger should not pretend to understand. Some feel that the unscrupulous priesthood have led their countrymen into this snare of folly to maintain their own supremacy.

Whatever may be the case, an Englishman says that caste in India is an interesting institution. It is quite natural that no other feeling than that of amusement should occur to the English mind. He can afford to laugh at the absurdities and contradictions in such an antiquated and complicated institution. The greater the folly in the institutions of the strangers, the greater is the enjoyment felt. The Englishman frames a nice little table-talk, with caste as his topic. An American missionary finds the subject very useful to induce his countrymen to subscribe money to save the souls of two hundred millions of people from heathenism.

The European and American people who write on caste do not necessarily do so to bring the folly to the attention of their countrymen for the purpose of ridicule. There are some strangers who look on this question with philosophic interest, but it is very little different from the interest felt by an entomologist observing the habits of ants.

But the sons of India would have to think on caste with quite a different feeling. They cannot afford to enjoy the absurdities as an Englishman would. They have to be serious. A scientific investigator who is not a Hindu would look at this Hindu society without any feeling, as a medical man would examine a dead body. But a Hindu cannot be so unmoved. The more he thinks on the caste system, the better he understands his own burden. As one looking at a cancer would like to turn away his eyes, so a Hindu would like to discontinue his thoughts. But such dislike he must not entertain even for a moment. However pleasing might be the bliss of ignorance, the price which is to be paid would make us drop the idea of tasting such bliss. Investigation in this problem must be carried on without any feeling. It is a critical moment, a question of life and death, and we ought to consider it, and there is no way to escape.

Those who look at the caste distinctions and the evil consequences may even feel that this ship of caste has gone out of control. All that I can say is that we have no reason to despair. Methods of investigation which enable us to ascertain causes and extent of an evil, and to adopt proper remedies therefor, are making more rapid progress to-day than ever before, and the work which the great men of the past have done is before us, and we can avoid their mistakes. All the attempts made by the previous workers to break this caste system have failed, but it should not be thought that all the possible remedies have been exhausted.

We ought to investigate what the condition to-day is, how it came to be, whether it is desirable; and, if not desirable, what methods, if any there be, can be adopted to get out of such a condition.

My intention in this study of caste may here be stated. It is not only to lay down a method for the study of caste and to find out the general principles of the present formation, but also to find how and when this snare came to be woven and to see whether its history suggests any methods to remodel it.

People of superior intelligence and authority have made several attempts to do what I am proposing to do, and have failed. I am not quite sure whether the remedies which I shall suggest would be crowned with success, but I shall lay before the readers the results of my investigations.

This book is especially for the Hindus, but I do not at all expect that it will be acceptable to all. I do not pretend to write for those who believe that the caste system must be good because it was introduced by our forefathers and because our forefathers were wiser than we are and that we are in the wrong if we think it bad. Nor do I write for those who believe that the great sages who gave the law in the past ages were omniscient and that a frail mortal of to-day ought not to criticise their writings.[1] But I write this book for those

---

[1] Such attitude is shown by some very prominent orthodox Brahmins. See for example the sentiment expressed in the preface of Arvâchîna Kosha by Godbolé.

who, with best respect for those sages, are prepared to admit that those sages were men, and that they were liable as men to err, and that, if they have erred, it is neither a sin nor an impossibility to correct them.

The European scholars who study this question concentrate their attention on understanding the present. Some of them see the need of considering how this institution came into existence; but they rarely care to consider what a thoughtful Hindu thinks about, namely, the future of caste and the possibilities of modifying it. Whether they consider this or not, it cannot be deemed unnecessary for them to think. As long as caste in India does exist, Hindus will hardly intermarry or have any social intercourse with outsiders; and if Hindus migrate to other regions on earth, Indian caste would become a world problem. An outsider going to India and staying there for centuries would remain an outsider and could never be assimilated. To the gradual unification of the world, one-fifth part of which is entangled by the caste system, there is no other single obstacle of equal magnitude. How great the problem before the Hindus is, is hard for the European to understand. The people of the United States, where two castes prevail, would be able to understand the magnitude of this problem to a slight degree. It would be a good thing for this republic if the scholars here would take a little more of scientific attitude toward the situation in India instead of joining with the European writers in censuring us for this institution, when we ourselves well understand it to be defective but do not know how to improve it.

To state the difficulties in our way, suffice it to say that caste is a development of at least three thousand years, and all the social manners and customs of the Hindus are so modeled and interrelated as to fit the caste system. The more highly organized a system, the harder it is to change, and the caste system is no exception to this rule. We find revolts against this system from the very earliest period up to to-day, and most of them succeeded only in multiplying the evils. Principles antagonistic to the system were forced into society by the swords of the Mohammedans, by the bayonets of the Portuguese, and by the organized missions of Europeans and Americans of the nineteenth and twentieth centuries, but they all failed to make any impression.

The extent of the work which we have to do is also a matter to be seriously considered. Of the three hundred millions of people in India, two hundred millions are Hindus, and eighty millions are Mohammedans. The two hundred million Hindus are made up of diverse racial elements, speak about nineteen developed languages, and over one hundred dialects. They are again divided into over three thousand castes, most of them having subcastes. One of these castes, *i. e.*, that of the Brahmins (Brāhmaṇas),[2] is divided into over eight hundred subcastes. None of them intermarry and most of them do not dine together.

The extent of the prejudices which we have to overcome is by no means a negligible factor. The social distance between man and man is too great for a Westerner easily to imagine. A Brahmin is a holy man, while

[2] The correct Sanskrit word is Brāhmaṇa. Brahmin is a popular English corruption of that word.

a Mahar is foul and untouchable. Between them we find a series of castes of countless gradations. The words "foul and untouchable" need some explanation. If a Mahar touches, or even if his shadow falls on a Hindu of a good caste, the latter is supposed to be polluted and is himself unfit to be touched or to enter a house unless he takes a bath. How to simplify these social relations is the problem for us to solve.

To effect any change in a society so complex and so highly organized, a tremendous force is needed, and where is it? It might be thought that individuals might get over these notions of their own accord and remove the evil, but that idea would prove fallacious. Individuals, especially of the higher castes, do not suffer very great inconvenience in their actual dealings, though society as a whole is weakened by the system. As they do not find any inconvenience by letting the things go on as they are going now, they have no inclination to work in the opposite direction and get into trouble. When individuals cannot remove an evil it is the duty of the community or government to do it. The government of India does not care to reform society, because it is afraid that its intentions may be misunderstood. It has determined on a policy of letting society alone.[8] The task will fall upon some disinterested people who look to the

[8] It is very sad that the government of India denies the natives of the country any share in the government, when it is unfit to make any social reforms itself. It is vain for an Englishman to blame the Hindu for his caste when the former has so resolutely kept the instrument of progress and reform away from the Hindu. It is an irony of fate that the Englishmen who push a bill in the House of Commons on most trifling questions expect the natives of India to do all the social reform without the aid of government and the legislature.

I have given in the seventh or last chapter the discrimination on the lines of *varna* as advised by the text. Here I have tried to ascertain the actual facts of the period, using the text as a material, and have taken its testimony with all due limitations. I have tried to find out how far *varna* of the party was considered in the questions of treatment at the court, taxation, inheritance, marriage, and the criminal law.

While discussing the caste system in India, I have incidentally made a few references to the caste system in the United States. These references should not in any way be construed as an attempt on my part to find fault with the Americans and their civilization. I have made these references primarily to make the Indian conditions clearer with the aid of phenomena which are more known and likely to be more easily observed by the Western World. I also trust that these illustrations will point out how a people even with the noblest ideals before them and making huge efforts to maintain those ideals, cannot entirely escape the consequences of events somewhat beyond their control. It may also happen that the mention of these similarities may enable the people of this republic to understand the Hindus a little better.

CHAPTER II.

THE CASTE SYSTEM.

1. *Definition of Caste.*

The word "caste."—This is of Spanish and Portuguese origin. Casta means lineage or race. It is derived from the Latin word Castus, which means pure. The Spaniards were the first to use it, but its Indian application is from the Portuguese, who had so applied it in the middle of the fifteenth century. The current spelling of the word is after the French word "Caste," which appears in 1740 in the "academies," and is hardly found before 1800. Before that time it was spelt as "cast." In the sense of race or breed of man it was used as early as 1555 A. D.[1] The Spanish word "Casta" was applied to the mixed breed between Europeans, Indians (American) and negroes.[2] But "caste" was not used in its Indian sense till the seventeenth century.[3] The Indian use is the leading one now, and it has influenced all other uses. As the Indian idea of caste was but vaguely understood, this word was loosely applied to the hereditary classes[4] of Europe resembling the castes of

[1] Their (of the Nabatheens) caste is wittye in winning of substance Fardle Facions, II, i, 118.

[2] Faun & Ulloa's *Voyages to South America.* (1772) I, 1, iv, 29.

[3] Examples of use in this sense are "The Banians kill nothing and there are thirtie and odd severall casts of these." Purchas *Pilgr.* i, 485(Y). (1613 A. D.); "The common Brahmins have eighty-two casts or tribes, Lord *Banian,* 1630 A. D.

[4] Her manners had not that repose
Which stamps the caste of Vere de Vere.
[Tennyson's *Lady Clara Vere de Vere.*]

India, who keep themselves socially distinct. Darwin[5] has applied this word to different classes of social insects. The Portuguese used this word to denote the Indian institution, as they thought such a system was intended to keep purity of blood. We thus see that derivation of the word does not help us to understand what caste is.

Definitions of a caste by other writers.—Before giving my own definition of a caste, I shall give the definitions by other writers. They may be found in the various volumes of the Report of the Census of India for 1901. M. Senart has written an admirable book in French. In his book, "after reminding his readers that no statement that can be made on the subject can be considered as absolutely true, that the apparent relations of the facts admit of numerous shades of distinction, and that only the most general characteristics cover the whole of the subject, he goes on to describe a caste as a close corporation, in theory at any rate rigorously hereditary; equipped with a certain traditional and independent organization including a chief and a council, meeting on occasion in assemblies of more or less plenary authority and joining together at certain festivals; bound together by common occupations, which relate more particularly to marriage and to food and to questions of ceremonial pollution, and ruling its members by the exercise of jurisdiction the extent of which varies, but which succeeds in making the authority of the community more felt by the sanction of certain penalties and, above all,

[5] The castes are connected together by finely graduated varieties. Darwin's *Origin of Species,* ii, 36 (1836 A. D.).

by final irrevocable exclusion from the group."[6] All that may be said in favor of the above cited words is that they are not a bad description of a caste, though the use of some of the principal words, like "close corporation," might be questioned. Again, all castes do not have councils.

Nesfield defines a caste as "a class of the community which disowns any connection with any other class and can neither intermarry nor eat nor drink with any but persons of their own community." Here Nesfield has given only one essential of a caste.

Sir H. Risley defines a caste as follows: "A caste may be defined as a collection of families or groups of families bearing a common name which usually denotes or is associated with specific occupation, claiming common descent from a mythical ancestor, human or divine, professing to follow the same professional callings and are regarded by those who are competent to give an opinion as forming a single homogeneous community."

There are some statements farther on which may be regarded as a part of his definition of a caste, and which may be summarized as follows: A caste is almost invariably endogamous in the sense that a member of a large circle denoted by a common name may not marry outside the circle; but within the circle there are smaller circles, each of which is also endogamous. What I have said about the definition of Senart may be said about this definition.

[6] Report of the census of India for 1901, vol. I. To my knowledge Senart in his book, *Les Castes dans l' Inde*, published at Paris, has brought for the first time to the attention of the European world the fact that a caste and a *varna* are not identical.

My own definition of a caste.—A caste is a social group having two characteristics: (1) membership is confined to those who are born of members and includes all persons so born; (2) the members are fobidden by an inexorable social law to marry outside the group. Each one of such groups has a special name by which it is called. Several of such small aggregates are grouped together under a common name, while these larger groups are but subdivisions of groups still larger which have independent names.

Thus we see that there are several stages of groups and that the word "caste" is applied to groups at any stage. The words "caste" and "subcaste" are not absolute but comparative in signification. The larger group will be called a caste, while the smaller group will be called a subcaste. A group is a caste or a subcaste in comparison with smaller or larger. When we talk of Maratha Brahmin and Konkan Brahmin, the first one would be called a caste while the latter would be called a subcaste; but in a general way both of them might be called castes. Maratha Brahmins in their turn would be called a subcaste of the southern or Dravidian Brahmins.

These divisions and subdivisions are introduced on different principles. In this way two hundred million Hindus are so much divided and subdivided that there are castes who cannot marry outside fifteen families. On the other hand, there are some castes in which the process of division and subdivision has not been carried to its logical extent which can boast of five million.

These three thousand castes with their subcastes put together make Hindu society. There is no intermarriage, and very little of social intercourse in its proper sense. The only uniting tie between these sharply differentiated bodies is a certain amount of common tradition, and common language for a number of them, and for all a common religion which consists in being disciples of the Brahmins.

There is a very strong feeling of caste-patriotism amongst all castes, even where patriotism in its larger sense exists. A Maratha Brahmin feels as strong a pride in being a Brahmin as he feels in being a Maratha; while in other parts of India a Brahmin feels pride in being a Brahmin, and in nothing else.

When I say that Hindu society is divided into so many castes it should not be understood that so many thousand castes have split out of one united body. A united body of people large enough to produce so many castes by subdivision never existed in India. Numerous tribes which were living in different parts of India existed as different units, and after the custom of endogamy was introduced they did not fuse, though scattered all over the country.

In Europe the tribes were as numerous as in India but they have fused together. European nations and the white Americans might be compared to a chemical compound, while the people of India may be said to be a mechanical mixture. Reasons for this assertion will be evident from the history of caste later on.

But it should not be understood that castes are made only out of tribes. Originally united bodies were also divided into many castes. The principles of division were class, occupation, religious denomination or brotherhood, nationality, locality, allegiance to a trade-guild, schools of Vedic literature, and many others.

I have already said that these castes are a hierarchy. Brahmins are at the top, while there are some castes which are untouchable and are at the bottom. Though there are castes of innumerable gradations, it should be remembered that it is practically impossible for individuals to change their caste.

The internal structure of a caste is not quite simple. Castes are again divided into several groups called gotras. These gotras are exogamous. They are something like the Roman Gens. All persons who belong to a certain gotra, like Kaushika or Garga, are supposed to be persons descended from the mythical ancestor Kaushika or Garga. No family may marry with a family of the same gotra. In general all the gotras or exogamous groups have the same status in the castes. But there are some castes where such is not the case. In some parts of India there is hypergamy. Certain groups of families in a caste are considered higher than the rest, and it is customary that women in the inferior groups should seek to marry with men in the superior groups, but not vice versa. This kind of custom is confined mostly to Northern India, and is found in its worst form in Bengal.

Castes are to be distinguished in one point from the hereditary classes, like those of Europe who marry among themselves, that the people who are not born in those classes could rise to that class by their ability, while nobody can go into a higher caste. Among classes who marry among themselves, marriage outside the class is prevented by sentiment and not by hard and fast rules. Marriage outside the class in Europe might be rare or invalid, but in India if it is contracted outside the caste it is a sacrilege.

When the word "caste" is used as an abstract noun it means either the caste system or any of its supposed peculiarities, like exclusiveness, hierarchy, fixed order of things, greater regard to the ancestry of a person than to his individual merits, pretensions of the purity of blood, feeling of superiority and inferiority or customary manifestations thereof. I have also noticed that many popular writers when they wish to express themselves strongly use this word to denote classes or restrictions of any kind.

"**Origin of caste.**"—This phrase has no meaning. As long as we use the abstract noun "caste" in a variety of senses and the words "caste system" as one expression to denote a group of phenomena, the expression "origin of caste" can have no meaning. The theory of four classes (var*n*as) in society has its origin; sharp lines between various layers of society have their origin; ascendency of the priests and their exclusiveness have their origin; association of purity and impurity to various objects also has its origin. We can even conceive of the origin of endogamy. If historical psychology should ever be worked out it may give us the origin of pride and of feelings of superiority and inferiority. Though each of these various phenomena can have an origin, the origin or genesis of caste or caste system cannot be conceived of as long as these words remain a collective expression. If we cannot control our fondness for the word "origin," we should better use the plural form, viz., "origins of caste;" this expression would have some meaning. It is the duty of the historian of caste to take into account all the complexities which make the caste system, and to go into the origin and the history of every one of them.

Caste and tribe.— When a wild tribe of India got itself adopted into Hindu society by becoming endogamous and by accepting Brahmins as its priests and by worshipping Hindu gods, then it became a caste. When the tribe is in process of transition the rule of endogamy is very lax.

Caste and occupation.— To-day a man can take to any occupation without changing his caste. The only exceptions are that nobody of a good caste would like to take to the occupation of shoemaker or scavenger, and no man who is not born a Brahmin would be accepted as a priest in the community.

2. *Theory of Caste.*

I have used this expression so as to include not only the principles on which precedence is based, and which are observed by Hindu society when questions of caste are decided, but also the axioms which are regarded as true. In this chapter I shall try to state those principles and to explain them if necessary, but shall refrain from any comment or criticism.

Hindus believe that all men in the world are divided into four castes: Brāhma*n*as (priests), Kshatriyas (warriors), Vaishyas (common people), and Shūdras (servants). The precedence of these castes is in the order of enumeration. All other castes are produced by intermarriage either with pure or the mixed. These differences in the castes are innate and can not be obliterated or concealed.

If there are any tribes or communities or nations like the old Greeks and English people where caste is not found, it is because those people neglected the rules of marriage and conduct, and have consequently merged into barbarism, and caste among them is destroyed by indiscreet intermixture (fusion of varnas).

The caste system does not decide the position of the Hindus only; it decides the position of non-Hindus in society, *e. g.*, the Mohammedans and Christians have a certain definite status according to Hindu social theory.

Caste is due to the occupation which a man's forefathers were in.

Nobody can raise his caste in the Kali age, the age of discord, while it was possible to do this in the good old Krita age, the age of virtue.

The precedence given to a caste is not given by man; it is absolute, and the order is supposed to be known and fixed, and it ought not to be otherwise.

Though no man can raise his caste, he can degrade it by neglect of the ceremonials or by connection with the "low and barbarous." In such case he may either degrade himself completely or hold an intermediate position.

As a man may lose his position in the caste, so a caste may lose its position in the society. Taking to low trades is one of the things which may cause such a degradation.

There are certain occupations considered higher than others. Among the occupations assigned to the people, the occupation of a writer is superior to that of a merchant; that of a goldsmith superior to that of a coppersmith, and so on.

Certain animals also have several degrees of status. varying from sacred and clean to unclean and foul. And the castes which serve these animals are graded accordingly.

A caste is again degraded by giving up or not having the traditional rules of purity of the surrounding dominant castes and by irregular conduct from their standard. In Western India, some castes are degraded by the use of wine and meat and even by that of tobacco. Many Brahmin castes in certain localities have lost in status by using meat, which is used in those localities only by non-Brahmins. Though the use of meat is generally not approved, yet the eating of beef and of pork and of vermin is considered most degrading. Many castes have been lowered in the social scale by the custom of polygamy, and by the custom prevailing among them of the purchasing the bride. They also gain or lose status according to the higher or lower form[7] of marriage which they use. Moreover, if at the time of the marriage the bride is already of age, that fact is considered as degrading to the caste. It is preferred that a girl should marry before she comes of age. The reasons for such a belief will be given later on.

These examples of the ceremonial law of purity, which tend to raise or lower the caste, are neither complete nor universal. The law differs according to the locality. The principles of ceremonial purity which in some parts form a hard and fast rule may be simply a sentiment elsewhere. When a question of precedence between two castes came before the colleges of Pundits in Benares, or Poona, it was decided, not by the observation of actual social conditions, but by the authority of old books.

7 The Hindu Scriptures distinguish eight forms of licit marriage.

When they did not find any reference to the caste in the old book, they would either identify it with some old caste, or might invent some explanation regarding its origin. When they admitted the pretensions to a higher status of a few castes, they depended not on the actual conditions, but on some fiction which was supposed to be misunderstood till then.

The underlying theory was that the laws which define caste status are fixed and known. They are given by the gods. It is the duty of the Pundits to explain the laws.

The question referred to the colleges of Pundits was usually this: Is the claim of a certain caste to being Brāhma*n*a or Kshatriya a true claim or a false one?

But every caste decides for itself whether certain members who have been guilty of irregular conduct should be allowed to remain in the caste, and also whether another caste is fit for intercourse with them and to what extent it is. Consequently, whatever opinion the colleges of the Pundits may give, the actual precedence depends on what a caste can exact. The Sarasvat Brahmins in Mahārāsh*t*ra, however, succeeded in proving their claims to Brahminship in the Peshwa's court; but since public opinion was against them, they did not get the status equal to that of other Brahmin castes.

But what does the precedence amount to? This precedence means simply a public opinion that one caste is better than another. It is this public opinion which is fought for even to-day. At present this caste precedence means very little tangible good. But under native rulers it may have been a tangible good. The country is now fallen into the hands of "casteless barbarians," and only formal precedence has remained.

The ways in which this precedence is manifested are worthy of notice, especially because, if we want to understand *de facto* and not *de jure* precedence, these ways are the only means to understand it.

How is the precedence manifested? As Brahmin is at the head of society holiness is the standard. A caste is pure or impure as much as it is high or low. This purity is not the outside purity, which is apparent to the "bodily eye," but it is some mystic, innate purity. If the pure and impure are brought together, the pure become impure. For this reason the holy and pure castes should keep as little connection with impure castes as possible. The purer the substance, the more easily it is soiled. So a caste should define its relation with another caste, in so far as the latter is pure or impure.

It should be remembered that there is a wide range of substances which are polluted by the touch of low castes. The higher caste may not take them when polluted. What substances are pure and what are impure, what substances are easily polluted and what are not, depends on the local customs. In the Maratha country, a Brahmin will regard water touched by any other caste but his own as polluted. In Gujarath and Bengal, a Brahmin may take water touched by a Shūdra. In the Maratha country, it is only the touch of the lower castes which pollutes food. But soldiers from many northern castes are known to throw away their food simply because the shadow of an English officer falls on it. The pretensions of Madras Brahmins go farther than that: their food is polluted if a man of low caste looks at it.

The theory of purity and pollution would require a whole volume to treat at length; but what I have already said will enable the reader to understand the justice of some of the rules which can be inferred, in order to understand the status of the caste. The rules are as follows:

(a) Where a certain caste cannot eat food cooked by another caste, while the latter permits food to be eaten which was cooked by the first caste, then the first caste is superior to the second.

(b) If a Brahmin or other high-caste Hindu keeps more connection with one caste than another, then the former is superior to the latter. For example:

i. If a Brahmin accepts water from another caste, that caste is considered as clean in Bengal.

ii. If he accepts food cooked in oil, then the caste is better.

iii. If he accepts food cooked in water, then the caste is still better.

(c) The amount of pollution that a caste carries with it makes the caste low or high. If a caste pollutes some substances, but not the rest, that caste is better than one which pollutes all substances. All three classes of castes stated under (b) are clean castes, which do not pollute water; but below them are castes who pollute water, and below them there are the following castes in the descending order of status:

i. Castes which pollute an earthen vessel.

ii. Castes which pollute a brass vessel.

iii. Castes which pollute the courtyard of the temple if they enter.

iv. The castes which pollute the town if they live in it, and are consequently required to live outside.

There is another shade of distinction regarding the grades of castes whom a Brahmin can touch or from whom he may, as in some parts, accept water without pollution.

(1) If a caste can give water to a Brahmin or touch him, that caste is pretty good.

(2) If a caste can give water to a Brahmin lady or touch without polluting her, that caste is better still.

(3) A caste from whom a Brahmin widow may accept water, or one whose members she can touch without being polluted, is the best of all.

I know that what I say looks very ridiculous; but if I explain the reason for these shades of distinction, then I think it will not look so ridiculous.

The harder the rules of ceremonial purity, the more easily they are broken. The more extravagant the notions of purity are, the more easily is the purity defiled. The castes are good in proportion to the hardness of the ceremonial rules of purity of the people they can touch without polluting them. The ceremonial rules of purity of a Brahmin lady are harder than those of men, and of widows harder than the ordinary women; and castes could be graded accordingly.

The Indian method of excommunicating a man also must be understood in order to understand the propriety of some rules regarding the treatment of the low classes.

If a man is excommunicated by his caste-fellows, nobody in the caste will marry with him or will accept water from his hands, or will invite him to dinner. Sometimes, if the offense is very bad, as the killing of a cow, the whole village will outcaste him. The priests will not attend any ceremonial in his house. The barbers will not shave him, and the washerman will not wash his clothes. These are the methods of bringing pressure on the man.

These ideas have their influence in manifesting the status of a caste. With these principles in view, the castes in some parts may be graded as follows: The castes served by good priests are superior to the castes served by degraded priests. Again, the castes served by a barber and a washerman are superior to those who are not. Even among the castes served by a barber, a distinction may be drawn based on the question whether the barber pares the nails or not; among the latter, whether he pares the toe nails or not. Nonperformance of service on the part of this powerful class implies inferiority in every case.

3. *Psychology of Caste.*

What human feelings lie at the basis of the mystery deserve to be considered. These social differences of caste have become so firm in the mind of the Hindu that he regards it as a very natural institution. An outsider regards it as foolish, harmful, unjust, and artificial. He thinks that the constitution of the Hindu's mind is different from that of all other people in the world.

How this caste distinction came into existence will be dealt with in the History of Caste. At present I confine myself to making a few remarks on whether there are any passions common to all human beings at the root of the caste system, or whether it is due to certain abnormal traits of character peculiar to a strange and unspeakable people, the Hindus.

I do not care to inquire into the reason of all the phenomena that are supposed to be a part or result of the Indian caste system. I make a few remarks regarding those that I consider most important. There are two important elements in the Hindu caste system; for example, endogamy and hierarchy. The classes, races, and occupations exclude themselves from other groups while there is an understanding that one group is superior to the other. Of these two let endogamy be singled for consideration.

I think that I should begin the discussion regarding the psychology of endogamy by quoting Westermark. He says: "Affection depends in a very high degree upon sympathy. Though distinct aptitudes, these two classes of emotions are most intimately connected: Affection is strengthened by sympathy, and sympathy is strengthened by affection. Community of interest, opinions, sentiment, culture, mode of life, as being essential to close sympathy, is therefore favorable to warm affection. If love is excited by contrasts it is so only within certain limits. The contrast cannot be so great as to exclude sympathy."[8]

Human affection is generally restricted to those who are similar to them in these respects. People differing in race, religion, civilization and customs are also different in those essentials of close sympathy, and human affection is always guided by race and religion, customs or social position.

It is not true that these factors always restrict man's choice. Marriages do take place where these factors are not considered. But they are so rare as to be regarded

[8] Westermark's History of Human Marriage (1891), chap. xvi, 362.

as a romance, and people feel like writing a novel or an invective when such a case may occur.

The greatest number of castes which do not marry with each other are simply tribes converted into castes. The tribes when they were converted into castes were often fighting with each other in the early days, when the seed of caste distinction was sown. At present the various tribes and castes feel strong repulsion against one another, and this fact is a clear manifestation of our present savagery. What I say is very humiliating but it is nevertheless true. One subdivision of a caste feels strong repulsion to another subdivision, because among the latter the use of tobacco is customary; two sections of one caste do not intermarry and feel strong repulsion for each other because they use different kinds of shoes; two castes refuse to marry with each other to-day because their forefathers at one time quarreled over the boundaries of the village or over certain other questions, important or foolish. The primitive nations always have a very strong dislike for one another. "Savage nations are subdivided into an infinity of tribes which, bearing a cruel hatred toward each other, form no intermarriages, even when their language springs from the same root and only a small arm of a river, or a group of hills, separates their habitations."[9]

The castes are not simply developed tribes. Classes are converted into castes by becoming endogamous. Sometimes a section of the society becoming a hereditary class like the Brahmins and desiring to become exclusive does not deign to marry outside the class.

[9] Humboldt Personal Narrative, vol. iii, 26, as quoted by Westermark, chap. xvi, 365.

Endogamy in this case is due to vanity and want of affection between the different layers of the society. This feeling is coupled with the desire for keeping the blood pure when the pretensions of the upper layer sufficiently increase.

Nowhere are the different orders of society more distinctly separated from each other than in the South Sea Islands. In the Mariami group it was the common belief that only the nobles were endowed with an immortal soul and a nobleman who married a girl of the people was punished with death. In Polynesia the commoners were looked upon by the nobility as a different species of being. Hence in the higher ranks the marriage was concluded only with persons of corresponding positions; and if in Tahiti, a woman of condition chose an inferior person as a husband the children he had by her were killed.

But let us not take all the instances from barbarous times and barbarous peoples. Let us take the case of civilized nations in Europe. In Sweden in the seventeenth century marriages outside the class were punished. According to the German civil law the marriage of a man belonging to the high nobility with a woman of inferior birth is still regarded as disparaging and the woman is not entitled to the rank of her husband nor is the full right of inheritance possessed by her or her children.

Another characteristic of the caste system is hierarchy. The feeling of superiority and inferiority either is a cause of endogamy or even a result thereof. A race of people which regards itself as superior to another will not intermarry with one that is thought inferior. Conversely if two races of people come together and do not intermarry, one would have to assume inferiority to the other. When the Chinese first came to the United States they were filled with prejudice against the white people and therefore did not intermarry; the whites and the yellows are two mutually exclusive communities, and the yellows are compelled to assume an inferior position. In South Africa, when the Hindus migrated there, and on account of their caste notions did not intermarry with the English settlers, a feeling of superiority and inferiority of race which did not exist before that time came into existence. When two people come together and do not intermarry freely, a feeling of superiority and inferiority is sure to come into existence.

One interesting feature in the hierarchy of caste is the preëminent position which the priests hold. I intend to write a special treatise on the question as to how the Brahmins attained such a high position in Hindu society and managed to maintain it for so long a time. At present I only remind the readers that this supremacy of the priest is not confined to India. The extravagant claims which the priest makes are always coexistent with the primitive character of the people. In ancient Persia, as well as ancient Egypt, the priest was always at the top. In Europe, till the nations were emancipated from the temporal control of the Pope the clergy was always superior to temporal authority. Even to-day I have known of Christian missionaries in India who are not much behind the Brahmins of olden times in making pretenses to occult superiority and omniscience and exalted position over the ignorant masses that came in contact with them. The scholar holds the highest position in the society of China, and this is probably due to the same feeling of respect for learning.

The sectarian castes in India owe their existence to the same mental attitude which people of different religions have regarding intermarriage. Mohammedans and Christians do not intermarry. Even the adherents of different churches have been prohibited from intermarrying. In the Roman Catholic Church the prohibition of marriage with heathens and Jews was soon followed by the prohibition of marriage with Protestants. Protestants also originally forbade such unions.

If the psychological reasons for caste are the same for the Hindus as for other peoples, why is it, we may ask, that the people of India have so tenaciously held to those customs and other people have dropped them?

We must remember that India, unlike other countries, has kept the custom of early marriage still in vogue. There is no choice in the marriage arrangements. If young men and young women were to marry for themselves, the caste restrictions would become much shaken. The feeling of love would have become an incentive to break the rules. But as the marriages are arranged by the parents, the force of this feeling is not available. The feelings, notions, and calculations of the parents being the controlling factors in the Indian marriages, the custom of marrying within the caste is retained.

Something must be due to the nature of the people themselves. The people of India were for many centuries unprogressive and trying to live up to the ideal past. For their guidance they do not depend on their own intelligence but on the intelligence of the people who are dead and gone. They will not break a custom because they see no sense in it as an Englishman or an American of strong individuality will do, but will blame their own frail intelligence that they do not see the sense in it. They have almost the same respect for what is old as Christians might have for the words of Jesus.

In the theory of caste the reason why certain occupations should be considered as pure and certain others as impure is very easy to understand; but why certain castes which have early marriage should be preferred to the castes with late marriages is a matter not so very easy.

The question of the causes of early marriages is quite different from the question why is the custom of early marriage so much honored. Early marriage itself depends on several factors. The fact that early marriage is considered sacred is simply one of the factors. That the earlier marriage should be considered holier than the late marriage is due to the hyperbolic notions of the Brahmins regarding purity. Their theory regarding early marriage may be stated as follows:

A really faithful man or woman ought not to feel affection for a woman or a man other than the one with whom he or she is united. Such purity is compulsory not only after marriage, but even before marriage, for that is the only correct ideal of chastity. No maiden could be considered pure if she feels love for a man other than the one to whom she might get married. As she does not know whom she is going to get married to, she must not feel affection for any man at all, before marriage. If she does so, it is a sin. So it is better for a girl to know whom she has to love, before any sexual consciousness has been awakened in her.[10]

[10] History of the word "caste" is well treated in the Murray's *Dictionary on Historical Principles*. The information on various castes can be found in the different *provincial gazetteers* and *census reports*. There are also various private publications which give important information on various subjects. Discussion regarding theory of caste is made by different officers in India in the census volumes, and the method to grade caste by the manifestations of theory of purity and-pollution is discussed bv Gait in his report on Bengal castes. The question of endogamy has been well discussed by Westermark in his standard work on the *History of Human Marriage*.

CHAPTER III.

HISTORY OF INDIA.

(250 B. C.–250 A. D.)

In order to understand the text before us, it is advisable to review the course of events for the five centuries within which the work must have been written. The political events and other great changes in India which were taking place two hundred and fifty years before and after the beginning of the Christian era deserve our attention.

The great emperor Ashoka was dead by 230 B. C. Within fifty years of his death the Maurya dynasty was overthrown. The dynasties of Shungas and Ka*n*vas, of whom very little more than a list of kings is known, appeared and disappeared within the next hundred and fifty years. During the rule of these two dynasties, the kingdom or the empire of which Pā*t*aliputra was the capital dwindled into insignificance. The empire had lost its hold in the Punjab, and the mastery of the province was left to be contested for by rival Greek potentates. The Andhras of the south, who had once paid tribute to the Mauryas of Pā*t*aliputra now raised their heads. They followed a career of conquest, pushing themselves farther and farther to the north, overthrew the Ka*n*vas and annexed their territory. The exact duration of the Andhra's authority in the north is a matter very uncertain. This dynasty terminated its existence about 236 A. D. according to the statements of the Matsya and Vāyu Purā*n*as, as interpreted by Vincent

Smith. The history of the northern as well as the southern divisions of India for one century is almost unknown. The country appears to have been given to anarchy in the third century.[1]

More information than this can hardly be given about the Magadha empire, and it is to be greatly regretted, because this empire was the most important part of India from the standpoint of the growth of dharma, in which we are specially interested. "For while in the western part of India, the coins have preserved the names of the kings, in Magadha the people continued to use the coinage bearing only private mark or marks of the individual or the guild that issued them. None of the ancient sites there, Sāvatthi or Vesāli or Mithila, Pātaliputra or Rājagaha, have been excavated, and thirdly the literature of Magadha mostly Jain or later Buddhist lies also still buried in the MSS."[2]

During the same period the province of Punjab by no means enjoyed any peace. Magadha was undergoing a change of dynasties and was suffering from the attack and rule of another power at home, but the Punjab was suffering from foreign invasion.

Seleukos Nikator, the great general of Alexander, who had become the emperor of a large part of Western Asia after the conqueror's death, was also dead. While Antiochus his grandson, a worthless man, was occupy-

[1] To this anarchy during the third and fourth centuries in southern India, Rājavāde attributes the corruption of the Mahārāshtri language, which led to the disappearance thereof, and to the rise of the present Marathi. (Vishva Vritta Magazine, Kolhapur, India, No. 3.) It is not improbable that a similar process was going on all over India and here may be found the origin of the present vernaculars.

[2] Rhys Davids, "*Buddhist India,*" xvi.

ing the throne, the empire was split into pieces, by the revolt of the Bactrians and the Parthians, both of which peoples had virtually become independent by 250 B. C.

The Bactrians had adopted Greek civilization, and were probably fused with the Greeks. They were consequently called Greeks (Yavanas). The hero of the Bactrian revolution, Diodatus, conquered some parts of India, namely, Kabul, Punjab, and Sindh. Though victorious in India, he lost his control over Bactria, which was wrested from him by his general Eukratides. Soon after this event, Eukratides was murdered and Bactria fell to pieces and into a number of small principalities. Menander was the chief of one of them and his invasion is probably referred to by Patanjali. This king was Buddhist and he is identified with King Milinda, so well known in Buddhistic literature. These Greek princes were fighting amongst themselves in Bactria as well as in the northwestern part of India for the mastery of the soil.

"While the Greek princes and princelings were struggling in obscure wars which history has not condescended to record, a great deluge was preparing in the steppes of Mongolia which was destined to sweep them all into nothingness."[3] The Shakas or the Scythians, who were a horde of nomads, broke loose on Bactria in the period between 140 and 130 B. C., and extinguished the Greek monarchies north of Hindu Kush. Some of these tribes entered India and made settlements at Taxila and

[3] This quotation from Vincent Smith's should not be construed as a commitment, at least on my part, that I believe the Shakas or the Scythians to be of Mongolian race. See *Proceedings of the Berlin Academy for 1908.*

Mathurā, and ruled there for more than a century seemingly in subordination to the Parthian power. Another section of the Shaka horde or the Parthians themselves occupied the peninsula of Surāshtra or Kathiawar, and established a dynasty of satraps there, which lasted for centuries. Another tribe of Scythians, cognate with Shakas and called Kushans, entered India by the beginning of the Christian era, and conquered Punjab and Kabul. King Kanishka of this tribe is well known. It appears that the Kushan dynasty held its own for a long time, as we hear of them as late as 360 A. D.

The Bactrian Greeks were not gone. Some of their tribes remained in India as a fighting element till very late. If they did not remain there, some other warlike foreign tribe which passed by their name "Yavanas" did remain. We find references to them along with Shakas and Pahlavas, in the Andhra inscription of 126 A. D. of the Chaitya cave at Nasik.

The narration of these few facts will make it sufficiently clear that during these five centuries the country was infested by foreigners. It should also be noted that some of these foreigners were Buddhists, some Brahminists, while some were observing outlandish beliefs and practices. Again for a considerable period the foreigners were dominant, and probably stayed in India permanently. Their relation with the Hindu society, or their position in the Hindu social system, must have been in the process of adjustment during this period. Hindu society, as it appears ultimately, had to assimilate this element.

Another peculiarity of this period was closer relations between the North and the South. It is true that some intercourse did exist between the two parts of the country before this period. Some adventurous princes like Rama of Kosala, and those of the Maurya dynasty, had ventured to the south to Vindhya. Brāhmanas had already migrated and carried their civilization and influence along with them, but the intercourse was not great enough to make the Northerners adopt a definite sentiment toward people and customs of the South. During the period under consideration, Andhras invaded and conquered a part of the North. This probably was the first attempt of the Southerners to rule the North, since the Rig Vedic immigration. Andhras were waging wars with Kathiawar, and thus exerted a considerable influence in India. They made their language Mahārāshṭrī a literary tongue and brought it among literary circles, to an importance second to Sanskrit alone. A sentiment in the North regarding the South was in the state of formation, and was to find its expression in their code of dharma doctrines.

Before the beginning of this period Buddhism had already passed the stage of mere theological doctrine and had grown up to a stage of heresy. During the period under consideration it probably was in the way of becoming an independent religion. The inherent weaknesses of the system, which was fated to disappear and deserved to disappear[4] from the land, were becoming apparent during this period. Still it was a factor

[4] I am stating here rather frankly the position I hold. I have in many places noticed some sentiments and opinions, rather timidly expressed, but which amount to something like this: "Buddhism was a very noble religion, which the Brāhmana scoundrels selfishly drove out from their land, and the people were big fools to let this good, noble religion disappear."

to be considered, and the relation of the heresy to the social changes was being made known, and principles were being laid down to deal with this creed.

If the political history of the five centuries under consideration is defective, the economic history of the period is still more so. In order to throw some light on this period, we should pay some attention to the economic achievements of India in the period that preceded.

Apart from agriculture, the people were following various other occupations. We hear of about eighteen guilds of different trades. Each guild (pūga or seniya) was presided over by an alderman or a president (a je*th*haka or a pamukha). These guilds not only attended to business disputes but also attended to disputes between members of the guild and their wives. There was a president-general (Mahāse*tt*hi) who decided disputes between guilds. The guilds or private individuals issued coinage, as well as credit instruments. There were no banking facilities and the custom of hoarding was common. The trade was done by caravans. There

Timid scholarship is not so frank in its statements, but the school of social reformers in India, which does not hold it to be its duty to be critical, has expressed such opinions more candidly. It is a pity that men holding even the highest judicial offices in India are so without knowledge of Brahminism and of Buddhism that they sometimes express without scruples such opinions as that Shankara made a great mistake in crushing out Buddhism. Very often Gautama is hailed as a breaker of caste system, while in fact he was no better than the present social reformers in ability to break it and much worse in his intentions and motives and policy, with reference to this question. I do not wish to make a digression here on this point, but shall do justice to the subject in my monograph on "Buddhism and Caste."

were no bridges; the roads were unsafe; and the caravans were protected by companies of volunteers, who hired themselves out. The king levied taxes as well as octroi duties. The custom of haggling for the price prevailed. In the case of goods ordered for the palace, there was an officer called valuer of goods, who attended to it. There were some important roads, for example from Sāvatthī to Rājagaha. from Videha to Gāndhāra, from Magadha to Sauvīra, we also hear of sea-voyages from Bharukachcha or Broach to Burma and to Babylon (Baveru)[5]

The philosophy of the period.— Something is necessary in the way of reviewing the philosophical thought of this period. The history of philosophical literature by dates is in a very rudimentary condition and consequently a sharp demarcation of the philosophical thought of this period from the thought of the period that preceded cannot be attempted. But inasmuch as the thought that preceded was in a large measure incorporated into the philosophy of these five centuries, such an attempt is needless.

To introduce the different mazes of philosophical systems would hardly be possible or wise even in the case of those which are most important. There are about

[5] These statements are taken from the article of Mrs. Rhys Davids. The learned lady has constructed this article with the Jātaka tales as the evidence. Now it will be readily admitted that the tales which Buddha told were very old tales even in his days, and from this it may be argued that the civilization which Mrs. Davids describes, belonged to a period much earlier. This objection may be partially true; still, one would find that Gautama, while narrating the tales which he told, modified them to suit the audience by introducing familiar spots and conditions.

sixty-two different doctrines mentioned in Brahminical and Buddhistic literature. Of these about eight systems are well known. Of these eight systems six are called orthodox systems as they all recognized the Vedas as infallible. The two remaining systems were those of Chārvakas and Buddha. The system of Chārvakas held that there is no god, no soul, and the writers of Vedas are liars, and sacrifice is a big folly, man should avoid pain, try to enjoy the world's pleasures and should not bother about future life. The Buddhists denied the infallibility of Veda, though their denial was not quite as honest as that of Chārvakas. They developed an independent line of thought which is well known. The six other philosophical systems better known as the six schools of philosophy were: i, Pūrva mīmānsā; ii, Uttra mīmānsā; iii, Sānkhya; iv, Yoga; v, Nyāya, and vi, Vaisheshika. All these systems believed in the infallibility of the Vedas. They differed from each other on the view of origin of the world. Some regarded that the world is a product of atomic agglomeration through activity. Some held that all the world is nothing else but Brahma. The fact it looks different to us is an illusion, yet illusion itself is a product of Brahma. The rest of them believed that matter, consisting of threefold essences (Gu*n*as), good, moderate, and bad, was converted into this subjective and objective world through the stages of perceiving and self-consciousness. These systems again differed from each other on the sources of true knowledge, like perception, inference, authority, etc. They had worked on different lines of thought; for example, Nyāya philosophy was mainly logic, Vaisheshika was metaphysics, Pūrva mīmānsā was philosophy of the interpretation of dharma from the Vedas. Vedānta and Sānkhya are more of pure philosophy. All these schools accepted the work of other schools in so far as it agreed with their own concepts.

All these different philosophies evolved greatly from the Vedic literature and Upanishads. Their history by periods cannot be written, the dates of three of the different promulgators are entirely unknown, and the original work of these promulgators is not extant in all cases.

Still it would not be a very bad presumption to say that these different systems were in the process of formation during these five hundred years under consideration. The relation of these systems to Mānava dharma-shāstra will be dealt with at the proper occasion

The intellectual activity of the period was not confined to philosophical discussion. Patanjali's famous work on Grammar appeared during this period. Garga's work on astronomy from which Varāha-mihira has so largely borrowed also appeared during this period.

We have reasons to conjecture that the epic of Mahābhārata was in the process of development during this period. Perhaps several of the Puranas also may have been compiled in some form or another. A considerable Jain, and Buddhistic literature came into existence during this period.[6]

[6] Materials for the history of the period. The political history of the period has been well worked out by Vincent Smith in his "*Early History of India, including Alexander's Campaigns.*" Oxford, 1904. He has written a very good monograph on the Andhras. Some different phases of the history have been touched by Rhys Davids in his "*Buddhist India.*" G. P.

Putnam's Sons, New York, 1903. Some attention to the economic history of India has been paid by Zimmer, Fick, and Hopkins. I have borrowed my information mainly from the "*Notes on Early Economic Conditions in Northern India.*" Article xxxi. J. R. A. S., 1901. The most popular work of R. C. Dutt, "*Civilization of Ancient India,*" vols. i, ii, should always be consulted, even though some of its views are out of date. There is a very useful work of reference by Mrs. Rickmers (C. Mable Duff) on "*Chronology of India.*" This book is written with great care. It gives references to various criticisms, discussions and dissertations, published in the various magazines or the publications of the government of India. Max Müller's work on the "*Six Systems of Indian Philosophy,*" is as yet the best work on Indian philosophy in European languages.

CHAPTER IV.

THE BOOK: MANAVA-DHARMA-SHASTRA.

Textual criticism.—Before turning to the contents of our document, it is but proper to make a few remarks on the texts of Manu on which the following investigation is based. All European editions but one and all Indian editions[1] adopted the text which was used by the commentator Kullūka.

It has been found that Kullūka is a very late commentator, and the text which he used is considerably different from those texts which were adopted by earlier commentators. Of the extant commentaries, the one by Medhātithi is the oldest. Still, the available manuscripts of his work, being defective, cannot be entirely depended on. The commentary of Govindarāja is in a more satisfactory condition. The latter, though not as ancient a person as Medhātithi, is nevertheless one of considerable antiquity. With the aid of Govindarāja and to a certain extent of Medhātithi and some other commentators, Professor Jolly has attempted to restore the text and produce an edition independent of Kullūka. The first attempt toward the critical study of the text was made by August Loiseleur Deslongchamps (Paris, 1830). But it is safe to say that Jolly's edition deprives all the preceding ones of their value, as it is the result of far-reaching critical studies. Both the versions are made use of in the text. If attention is paid to the various

[1] The edition of Mandalika gives the various readings, but the editor has followed no principle rigorously in his attempt to restore the text.

shades of meanings, the difference between the two editions is indeed considerable; but for the purposes of this history, as will be presently noticed, the differences are comparatively of small significance, excepting in a few cases where I have considered both the readings.[2]

Contents of the book.—If viewed rightly, this book presents a very logical arrangement. The law of proper conduct was, according to Sanskrit writers, twofold. Proper conduct for every order (āshrama) and proper conduct for every var*n*a, a word whose meaning we will discuss later. Propriety of conduct for a person was supposed to be determined by his origin. Every creature was supposed to be endowed with some peculiar nature at the time of creation, and consequently the writer first deals with the creation at the very beginning of the book. That in introducing the account of creation at the beginning the author was influenced by the Purānas, which were becoming popular at this time, is a fact too plain to need further comment. Then he turns to duties of the four orders (āshrama). The dharma for the four orders (āshramas) is treated along with the duties for Brāhma*n*as, as the former was likely

[2] While preparing this monograph the various editions of the text, commentaries, and translations, that were available to me were as follows:

Texts with or without commentaries:
Deslongchamps's text, Paris, 1830.
Jones's text.
Gore's text and Kullūka, Bombay, 1887.
Jully's Manutīkā-sangraha, extracts from six commentaries, Calcutta, 1886.
Mandalika text and seven commentaries, Bombay, 1886.
Jolly's critical ed. Trubner, London, 1887.

Translations:
George Bühler, Sacred Books of the East, 1886.
Burnell & Hopkins, Trubner & Co., London, 1884.

to be followed by Brāhmaṇas only, though it was desirable for all other varṇas to do the same. Devoting the next five chapters to this subject, the writer then turns to the dharma for the king, wherein he includes all the civil and criminal law. This treatment takes up chapters vii and viii and most of chapter ix. He explains the dharma for Vaishya and Shūdra in the few concluding verses of chapter ix. It was a period when a dharma-writer could plainly see that it was not enough to explain dharma for four varṇas. There were mixed castes to be guided. He had also realized that none of the four varṇas could observe their respective dharmas in the times of distress. He again knew that people may happen to break the injunctions of dharma, and this problem also demanded treatment. For this reason, the writer takes up these three questions; and in the treatment of the last question he includes the theory and practice of penances, which brings us to the close of chapter xi.

All this was to be done for the sake of supreme bliss. For the proper comprehension of the rules governing the supreme bliss, he discusses the law of the transmigration of souls. After this is done, he treats doubtful points of dharma and then concludes the twelfth or last chapter of his work.

The method of presentation.—The examination of the contents of the book would be inadequate if we did not pay attention to the method of presentation. The method of presentation has its bearing on interpretation of the meaning of the author, and therefore the method deserves being known.

This book is written in a heroic metre instead of being

written in prose of sūtra style, as are the previous works of Baudhāyana and others. The language also is well suited to an epic, and some verses in this book are actually found in the epics. In several places the writer indulges in a play of words. He often indulges in immoderate language and description, which is in general ill suited for dharma literature (for example, his eulogy of the majesty of the Brāhmaṇas, strictures on women, and so forth). He often makes contradictory statements. When he is talking about the importance of a certain point, he is likely to depreciate other things which he might praise highly at other places. The older writers did not try to justify the precepts which they lay down, but our writer does so. In such cases he either gives Vedic authority or philosophic reasons.

Our author endeavors to pass his work off as that of somebody else, namely, Manu, and this motive has had a great deal of influence on the treatment. He nearly succeeded in deceiving the readers till the merciless historical criticism of modern times stepped in.

The method of interpreting the book.—After the textual criticism and general survey of the contents of the book, our next task is to understand the meaning of the author. To understand and interpret our author correctly is by no means an easy matter, as one may suppose. The book was written in Sanskrit, and contains many words for which there are no proper equivalents in English. Again, the meaning of words in the Sanskrit language was by no means stationary and consequently the exact meaning of words must be determined by careful inspection of the entire work. We again have to determine the oblique meaning of the author, taking fully into account his method of stating facts or giving precepts. Again, as this work shares the nature of a poem with that of a legal treatise, the meaning becomes more difficult to understand, and the facts become more obscure.

But before entering into such a criticism ourselves we should first see how the Sanskrit commentaries, of which there are about seven available, interpret the text.

The commentators are always people who have great respect for their author, and wish to interpret him in the best light. The various commentaries on Mānava dharma-shāstra generally try to paraphrase the text in easier language, and often give examples to make clear what they say. They are constructive. If there be any two verses which contradict each other, the commentators would make one of them applicable in a restricted sense,[3] or they may say that both are valid and any course of conduct may be followed Sometimes they notice the contradiction, point it out and then give it as a reason why the words must be interpreted more liberally.[4] They often warn us not to take the verses too

[3] Regarding the efficacy of muttering prayers the text says: "He who stands during the morning twilight muttering Sāvitrī, removes the guilt contracted during the previous night. But he who recites it seated in the evening destroys the sin committed during the day." (ii. 102.) Here the commentators Medhātithi and Govindarāja point out that only trifling faults can be expiated in this manner, otherwise the chapter on penances would be useless.

[4] Our text advises the king (vii, 189) "Let him station the commander-in-chief and the adjutant-general in all directions." Medhātithi, while commenting on this verse, remarks that, as the commander-in-chief and the adjutant-general are but two persons, they cannot be stationed in all directions, therefore their servants also must be meant.

literally, and explain the implied meaning.[5] They often compare a statement in the text with some Vedic text, in order to test the validity of the Mānava text.[6]

In order to illustrate a verse, Medhātithi quite often takes instances from the customs around him as he saw them.[7] He again points out at times any redundant words he may find.[8] Nor does he shrink from declaring many verses as arthvādas, which means that the moral only of the verse is to be believed.[9]

[5] Our text lays down a rule: "If a man has a wife, and with the begged money, weds a second wife, then the child (of the second wife) does not belong to the father, but to the giver of the money" (xi, 5). Govindarāja and Kullūka here warn us not to take the verse in a literal sense "The object of the verse is to forbid that alms shall be asked or given for such a purpose."

[6] When our text says (ix, 65) "that Niyoga or the appointment of the widows is nowhere mentioned in the Vedas, Medhātithi, while commenting on ix, 66, points out that the custom is mentioned in *Rig*-Veda x, 402.

[7] The text says (vii, 13). "Let no man therefore transgress that law which the king decrees with respect to his favorites, nor his orders which inflict pain on those in disfavor." In order to illustrate the rule Medhātithi gives the following instances. If a king orders that during the celebration of a wedding in the house of a minister or other favorite, a public festival is to be held in town, that everybody is to appear on the occasion, or, that during so and so many days no animals are to be killed, no birds are to be snared, no debtors are to be imprisoned by their creditors, then everybody must obey. The same shall be the case if the king orders with respect to persons in disfavor that they are to be shunned by everybody, that nobody is to enter their houses.

[8] In the text we find a precept that the names of women should be easy to pronounce, not imply anything dreadful, possess a plain meaning, be pleasing and auspicious, end in long vowels and contain a word of benediction (ii, 33). Medhātithi irreverently, but pertinently, remarks that there is no difference between auspiciousness (mangala) and benediction (āshīrvāda) and the latter word is added merely in order to complete the verse.

[9] Our text says (iii, 50): "He who avoids women on the six forbidden nights and on eight others, is (equal in chastity to)

What I have said regarding the attitude of the commentators toward the text will show that they were not, as is often urged, a class entirely wanting in critical spirit. Still, it must be admitted that their method of criticism was considerably defective. The main defect in their criticism is that it is not historical, nor did they aim to make it so. Their aim was not to produce a commentary for academic purposes, which would give the meaning of the text as it was understood by the author himself, but they wanted to explain the text in such a manner as would serve the needs of the society of their own time and place. Their attitude toward the text was the same as that of the judge toward the law, who really modifies it to suit new conditions under the pretense of interpreting it. If they want anything approved or condemned they approve or condemn it, provided they find any text which can be made to imply the desired doctrine;[10] and for this task they were very

a student (celibate), in whatsoever order he may live (*i. e.*, whether he be a householder or a hermit). Medhātithi remarks that this is merely an arthavāda and refers to no other order but that of householders. Govindarāja has turned this verse to account, to justify the return of sannyasin to household duties. He says that this verse permits even an ascetic who has lost all his children to approach his wife during two nights in each month. Kullūka ridicules this opinion, not being aware of the probable motives of Govindrāja in this interpretation.

[10] I think this was the attitude of Govindrāja (whom I think to be a Maratha Brāhma*n*a) when he interpreted i, 50, as a verse which permitted a sannyāsin to return to household duty. The event which warranted such an interpretation was I think the return to household duty by Vi*thth*ala the father of Jñāneshvara at the order of his teacher Rāmānuja who initiated Vi*thth*ala to the order, without knowing exactly the situation under which the young wife of Vi*thth*ala gave her consent. When the young wife of Vi*thth*ala paid her respects to Rāmānuja, the latter gave her a blessing that she would have illustrious sons. When he came to know that young lady's husband

well equipped. They were learned in Vedas, Mīmānsā and other philosophies and legal literature. Thus it will be noticed that the commentators cannot always be relied upon for the accurate meaning of the text. Not only their motive was one different than that of an historical critic, but so also was their method. First of all, the very respect which they may have for the author would lead them to give an interpretation much better than the author intended. They would try to reconcile contradictions which the author never noticed.

While explaining the meaning of the word, the commentators depended not so much upon the text itself, to find out how the author has used the word in several other places, as on the dictionaries already in use, like Amarakosha. Consequently, the various shades of meanings are not taken into account by the commentators. Evidently what the commentators may explain needs a check from critical scholarship.

Again, their glosses are inadequate for us. Some ideas which are peculiar to the period of the text have disappeared to-day. Again, commentators often write in the same kind of language as the text and do not bring to light the oblique meaning. Their aim being to guide society, they would be unwilling to have their text

who was no other person that his disciple Vi*thth*ala who had already become a recluse and the fact would prevent the fulfilment of his blessing, he ordered his disciple Vi*thth*ala to return to household duty. Thus when the couple were reunited they had three sons and a daughter, who won the respect and admiration of the whole country by their knowledge and saintliness. The Brāhma*n*as had ostracized these people for a time, for they were children of a sannyāsin. It is not improbable that Govindarāja made out a pecular meaning from the verse in order to remove the taint over the birth of the great man of his country.

lose all its force by explanation of the truth on their part. They would keep a fiction as it is; and for this reason, a thorough research should be made to get at the common stock of ideas. The motives which are likely to affect a dharma-writer either of the text or of the commentary, the philosophy by which they were influenced, the social background, ought to be studied; for without the aid of these, the expressions of the writers would be largely unintelligible.

At the period of our writer the Vedas had firmly established their position, the dharma-writers had come to a definite opinion regarding the eternity and infallibility of the Vedas. The sages who established new sciences and philosophy but who did not join the heresy were received with very great veneration among the public. Sciences like mathematics, astronomy, and medicine had assumed a semisacred character, as they were supposed to be based on the Vedas, and as such could not have been neglected by a dharma-writer. People followed not dharma alone, but all Shāstras, of which dharma was one. A shrewd scholar must have easily noticed that the incorporation of principles of other sciences into dharma would lead naturally to dharma's supremacy. The science or philosophy of ritual and sacrifice also had come into existence. The different schools of dharma were at variance, Purāṇas with their characteristic doctrines were coming forth, the doctrine of Buddhism had gained hold on the minds of the people. The authority of the Vedas and the habit of referring to the authority of books also was questioned, if not discredited, and consequently the application of the doctrines of philosophy or some kind of reasoning was becoming absolutely necessary.

Not only the condition of literature and development of thought called forth a readjustment of dharma, but new social problems were coming forth which were making such a task peremptory. New races and tribes were coming into contact with the standard population of Madhyadesha; the proper relation to be maintained toward them was to be treated by a work on dharma. Customs like Niyoga, or the appointment of widows, which were once valid, were falling into disrepute; new institutions were rising; economic conditions were becoming more complex; the ideas regarding purity and pollution were becoming more and more extravagant. All these facts were excuse and motive for a new work.

The motives of the author.— The motives with which the writer of our text appears to have been affected are mainly (1) a respect for tradition, which included Vedas, smritis, and other sacred or semisacred literature; and (2) a sense of inadequacy of the injunctions of the past; and (3) a desire for a more systematic arrangement, with some principles or philosophy in view.

But these were not the only motives which influenced our writer. The book of this author, as well as those of all other writers of dharma, were influenced by the inherent weakness of the politics of the country. The country was divided into numerous tribes, nations, or states; it was only when a powerful monarch would rise that a large part of the country would come under one head. Under these conditions, a positive law which would be obeyed by all people could not have been thought of. The thankless task of guiding the people and of preventing them from doing wrong fell, to a large extent, on spiritual authority, as the political authority was unfit for their share of the burden. More than this, for the welfare of the people the princes also were to be advised with reference to their own conduct, since they, without proper guidance, would have misused their authority.

But with such a huge task before the Brāhmaṇas. what power did they have? All that they had to rely on was their knowledge of the sacred literature, for which all people had high respect. Therefore, all that they could do to prevent improper conduct was to condemn it in strong language on the authority of the Vedas.

Again, the education of the people was very poor. Although the sciences and philosophies could develop, and did develop, without the art of writing, or at least without any extensive use of it, they could by no means be popular. Learning was confined to a small class of people who developed their mental powers very highly, while the masses were ignorant. The masses could not have been guided either by utility or by abstract moral principles. They were to be compelled to follow righteous conduct, either through the terrors of the regal sceptre or of hell.[11] All these facts had a determinate relation with the motives of the writer. When a dharma-writer tells us that a certain action leads to hell or to

[11] On the one hand, thought, perfectly free, freer and more liberal than in any other place in the world; and, on the other, gross superstition amounting to savagery, such is the contrast which the faith of the Hindu presents. This peculiarity is due to the extreme difference in learning which existed and exists in the various grades of society. Even to-day the intellectual classes of India will not compare unfavorably with the intellectual classes of any country, while the masses are still laboring in utter ignorance, and are kept orderly and moral, not by regard to civil and social ideals, but by beliefs such as the dharma-writings have spread.

such and such torments for the wrongdoer or his forefathers, it should by no means be considered that the writer was always a fool to think so, but only that he found it necessary to say so.[12] I have made the motives of the writer a subject of examination, not only to enable us to get at the facts more accurately, but also to better understand the personality of the writer. The author of a book which enjoyed such universal prestige in India should not suffer condemnation without reason. The facts regarding some of the statements he makes may be gathered from evidence independent of our text and without taking any care to determine the meaning and motive of its statements, but in such a case we are very likely to censure the author very unjustly as a producer of a work full of error, nonsense, contradiction, or fraud.

Place of the work in legal literature.—It has been well shown by Dr. Bühler, in his learned introduction to the translation of our text, that this text is a conversion of Mānava-dharma-sūtra, which itself belonged to the Maitrāya*n*iya school of Black Yajns. The text of Mānava-dharma-sūtra is yet unavailable. The manuscripts of G*r*ihya and Shrauta sūtras of this school are extant.

Dharma sūtras date from 600 to 300 B. C. They were manuals of conduct belonging to different branches of Vedas. Mānava-dharma-sūtra must have been a similar book, compiled at some time when other sūtras

12 Sometimes the great ignorance which Western writers display in interpreting the rules given in our text, becomes simply vexing, especially when they attribute false motives to the Indian priesthood.

were compiled. All these sūtras were of local validity, sectarian, unsystematic and incomplete. With the growth of society, a more comprehensive book, free from the defects mentioned, became necessary. The old and new parts of this work also have been ably determined by Dr. Bühler. He has very carefully gathered passages parallel to those of our text from ritualistic and dharma literature, two Upanishads, Nirukta, Mahābhārata and Vishnu Purāna, and has well discussed the source of additions which our writer must have made to the original Mānava-dharma-sūtra.

Dr. Bühler has also discussed the question whether the recensions before us is an immediate offspring of Mānava dharma sūtra or was a gradual growth; and he concludes that it was done at once. He has placed the book somewhere between 200 B. C. and 200 A. D.

Nature of dharma.— It has already been said that Mānava-dharma-shāstra is a work on dharma. In order to interpret the book properly, we should first consider the nature of dharma.

The science of Dharma first evolved as a division of Kalpa sciences which dealt with sacrifices and ceremonial, and which were divided into Shrauta sūtras (aphorisms which treat of the duties of a sacrificer), Grihya sūtras (sūtras teaching the duty of a householder) and Dharma sūtra (which teach the duties of a citizen). The field which should be occupied by Dharma in contrast with those of Shrauta and Grihya was not sharply defined. Subjects treated by Dharma sūtra of a certain school are treated by Grihya sūtras of another school and *vice versa.* Dharma had various shades of meanings. It meant law proper, rule of right, morality religion, innate quality, justice, and above all, duty. Later on, the meaning was restricted, and the ideas which were grouped under dharma became more and more definite. In Buddhistic literature the word "dharma" (dhamma), besides its common meaning, was also used technically in a philosophical sense, the elucidation of which is unnecessary for our present purposes.

In Brahminical literature the word "dharma" probably kept its field, but the different ideas which were denoted by it came to be better distinguished from one another. So dharma was divided into three branches: 1. Achāra dharma ("usages," rules of custom and ceremony); 2. Vyavahāra dharma, or (law proper), and 3. Prāyaschitta dharma (rules regarding atonement and penances). During the time of Mānava-dharma-shāstra, the threefold division was in the state of incubation, while in Yājñavalkya's times, these divisions appear to have been already made, as he has adopted this threefold division in his well-known smriti. The writers like Nārada and Brihaspati expound Vyavahāra dharma only, and we have a number of writers treating one or other of the threefold divisions.

These few facts will enable the reader to understand that the word "dharma" has a long history of its own and one almost entirely different from that of the word "law," the use of which in place of dharma would simply increase the confusion in the science.

Though the word has undergone various changes of meaning, one original idea contained in it was never lost sight of. Dharma never implied an order or command but a moral duty. The expounder of dharma was not the king but the priest. The king could not make or unmake dharma. It was absolute, eternal and unchangeable, while the priests were simply revealers or expounders. Sharing the nature of what we may call law, were the orders of the king of more or less permanency, but the king was supposed to issue them in accordance with dharma. As we know that the meaning of the word changed quite often, it is necessary for us to understand how the word was used by the writer of this sacred smriti. Fortunately he has discussed this subject in his own work.

The author has given his own ideas on dharma in the introductory verses of the second chapter. He says: "Dharma is something that is followed by learned men and assented to by the virtuous. It should be followed with the idea that the observance will bear fruit sometime, though it is preferable to follow it irrespective of reward. He who persists in discharging his duties in the right manner, reaches the deathless state. Vedas are the first source of dharma, next come smritis, and then the virtuous conduct of those who know the Veda and customs of the holy men, and finally "self-satisfaction." (This word carries a meaning similar to the word "conscience,") When two statements of the Vedas contradict each other any course of action may be followed."[13]

This explanation was enough for those who lived in India at the time when our text came to be written, but modern readers, who have forgotten the ideas and feelings which once prevailed, need some more explanation.

[13] Note the very great similarity of the description of dharma by Mîmânsakas.

I have already said that dharma was not what may be called positive law. Dharma was not a command of a political superior, but was in practice the advice of a spiritual superior. The expounder of dharma was not merely a jurisprudent but was primarily a teacher. This notion appears to be quite marked in the book under discussion. There we find the writer advising his reader what things would bring happiness to the latter and what will not. In order to elucidate the rules he often enters into elaborate discussion of the reasons for the respective statements, and shows their rationality. Another peculiar feature of dharma is law of preference, *e. g.*: A dharma writer would first give advice to the effect that everybody should marry in his own var*n*a; and again he would say that marrying a woman of lower var*n*a is permissible, while marrying one of higher var*n*a is never permissible. He would moreover urge that no Brāhma*n*a should marry a Shudra woman. There is something in the language of the book which will show clearly the fact that the rules given are precepts more than anything else. In India it is quite customary for a Brahmin to tell his son that to drink wine or to speak a lie is a greater sin than a murder and he would illustrate what he said by a story from a Purā*n*a. This should not be construed that the Brāhma*n*a does not understand the gravity of murder; it is rather merely a popular way of expressing the gravity of a certain action, by comparing it with actions the gravity of which is well recognized. We find statements of this nature and similar other exaggerated statements scattered all over the book.

Maintainance of dharma.—How was dharma maintained? The ceremonial part of dharma which was necessarily performed with the aid of Brahmanas was easily maintained, *e. g.:* The determination of the proper time for initiation of a certain caste. Here the Brāhmana was the person with whom the decision lay.[14]

Again the king was supposed to maintain dharma which the priest may declare to him. There was in general an understanding among the people, that dharma would be maintained not only by the kings, but also by the gods. The masses thus obeyed a large number of injunctions of dharma to avoid terrors of the future life. The transgressor would go to one or more of the twenty-one hells (iv, 87–90) or would be condemned to be born in the womb of lower animals (iii, 104) or barbarians. Not only himself but his ancestors (iii, 64–5, 92) or their manes (vi, 249) and descendants also would suffer. Adversity and diseases (xi, 49) would harass them who adhered to conduct not approved of by dharma as retribution for their sins.

[14] It should not be supposed that the people for whom the ceremonies may be performed by the Brāhmanas were always content with the decision which the Brāhmana might give. They often had aspirations of adopting a ceremonial belonging to a superior varna. Nor should it be supposed that the Brāhmanas with the fear of losing the patronage would always do what their patrons would say. When a certain caste called itself Kshatriya or Vaishya, the question must have been referred to a council of Brāhmanas, and what that council decided must have been accepted. If a Brāhmana did not abide by the decision he was ostracized. It is a mistake to suppose that the Brāhmanas were always easily influenced by money to perform any kind of ceremony. Even to-day I know of a Brāhmana of character sufficiently independent to give up all his Jahagīr of 40,000 rupees a year and refuse to perfom Vedokta ceremonies in the family of Shivajī.

A theory was already current that whatever a man enjoyed or suffered was a result of his own actions. His bad actions would bear him bitter fruit, whether they were done openly or concealed either in that birth or in the one next preceding. Not only was he dissuaded from bad life by the terrors of possible retribution but he was also persuaded into a meritorious life by promises of birth in a family of a Brāhmana or of a king, promises of absolution, of heaven, of expiation of sins of himself and also of his ancestors.

So peculiar a system to regulate the conduct would not have been complete without what was called Prāyaschitta or penance. This was primarily intended to expiate impurity, and to guard against retribution resulting from disapproved conduct. Punishments as well as penances had a power to free a man from guilt. When a man suffered a punishment for his wrong act, that wrong act would not affect his future, either in this world or the next, or in this life or the next. But punishments were too inadequate for the fulfilment of dharma. These penances were a necessary institution, to make amends for bad actions, of which the king did not take any notice, and also for offenses done secretly or remaining unpunished for various reasons.

Closely allied with these penances were austerities (Tapas), which if accumulated would guard a man from the chance of catching guilt in case he did wrong. These austerities became fruitless if the injunctions of dharma are broken.

The terrors of hell, the probability of having low birth, the penances, the likelihood of austerities being exhausted, the punishment by the king, all these were not enough to prevent a man from breaking the injunction of dharma. More terrible than all these was excommunication, which was intended to compel a man to observe the tribal or scriptural dharma. The method of excommunication did not differ very much in the times of our writer from what it is to-day: "Excluded from all fellowship at meals, excluded from all sacrifices, excluded from instruction and matrimonial alliance, abject and excluded from all religious duties, let him wander over this earth. These people should be cast off by their paternal and maternal relations, and would receive neither compassion nor salutation; that is the teaching of Manu" (ix, 238-9).

Date of the author.—Certain facts that can be gathered concerning the personality of the author now deserve our attention. The first question is the one regarding the date of the author. Dr. Bühler in his able introduction has given his estimate of the date to be some time between 200 B. C. and 200 A. D., and here I beg to differ from the learned critic. After examining the contents of the work carefully I have come to believe that the author could not have lived before 200 A. D., and am inclined to place him between 227 A. D. and 320 A. D.[1] For the proper treatment of the question I first summarize the reasons which induced Dr. Bühler to date the author when he did. Dr. Bühler admits that his estimate is based not on any direct evidence from the text referring to events whose dates are known, but is based on the relation-

[1] R. Pischel places our text in the second or third century A. D., but gives no reasons therefor. *Die Kultur der Gegenwart* (Berlin, 1906), part i, division vi, page 184.

ship of the text to documents whose dates are more or less known. Determining the position of our text in the legal literature, he has shown that the text could not have been written earlier than 200 B. C. and this of course is quite reasonable. The other terminus he thinks to be 200 A. D. and gives the following reasons:

(1) Nārada's work on law has been referred to in Harsha-charita by Bā*n*a who lived at the beginning of the seventh century (A. D.). Thus Nārada must have lived before Bā*n*a, while it is well known that the latter is himself much later than our text.

(2) Medhātithi, the writer of the oldest available commentary, lived probably in the ninth century,[2] knew of commentaries to which he was compelled to assign remote antiquity. Bühler thinks it only a moderate estimate if we assume that the earliest among them was about three or four hundred years old, and the glosses which existed in the fifth and sixth centuries show that even the earliest of them were separated by a considerable interval from the compilers of Manu-sm*ri*ti, an interval so great that the real meaning of the text seems to have been forgotten.

(3) The sm*ri*ti of B*ri*haspati which existed in 600 A. D., is found to be a Vārtika on Manu.

Besides these three principal arguments Dr. Bühler has given four others which, as he admitted, have a flaw of one kind or another.

Even a superficial examination of the evidence would

[2] The lower limit of Medhātithi's work is fixed by references to him made by Vijñāneshvara who lived in the eleventh century, and the remoter limit is determined by the reference to Kumarila Bha*tt*a, in the Bhāshya.

convince us of the fact that the lower terminus of 200 A. D. is only problematical. Even if we place the date of the document between 200 A. D.-300 A. D. these arguments would constitute no objection but would rather be a strong support.

Dr. Bühler discussed this question in the year 1886 and since then a good deal of lost history of India has been recovered, and consequently we are in a better position to judge the date of the author. In 1887 Professor Jolly published the text of Manu, and his edition is of great value to us in either raising or quelling the doubts about the possible interpolations in the book. Thus to-day we are enabled to study the question with greater advantage.

Arguments for the date of the author.—In the treatment of the mixed castes there are references in our text, regarding Andhras, Yavanas, Shakas Pahlavas, Lichchivis and Chīnas, which prove to be of great importance to us. We are assured that the references are not interpolations in the book, by the very fact that to make some statement about their status was a necessity and an excuse for a new treatise on dharma. The verses containing the references to these various peoples have been found in the Mahābhārata though in a slightly different form. Professor Jolly in his critical edition of the text does not regard them as interpolations. For these reasons I think that we can depend on these references to base our conclusions about the date of the author.

Our text describes Andhras as a tribe formed by the intermixture of Vaidehaka men and Kārāvāra women, and thus gives them a very low place, and says that they stayed outside the village and assigns them slaughter of wild animals as their duty or occupation (x, 36, 48). This description is very significant. He not only denies them the position of a Kshatriya but ranks them very low. Such a thing could not have happened when Andhras were in the ascendent. Since the death of Ashoka Andhras were rising steadily, so that in the year 27 B. C. they took control of Pā*t*aliputra. We are not certain as to how long the Andhra power lasted in the North. In the year 113 A. D., when Guatamīputra Shatakar*n*ī, who was an Andhra monarch, describes in his inscriptions his prowess and territories, the inscriptions show that he did not have any possession in the North at that time. It is possible that the Andhras may have been a ruling tribe in the South and a writer in the North may not have given them a very high place, but even such a thing does not seem probable as long as the Andhras were very powerful in the South, and well known in the country. But only when a dynasty was declining, as this was about 200 A. D. (it ended in fact in 227 A. D.), such a thing could be written safely, and a doctrine of this kind regarding the great nation in the South could have received currency.

We again have Yavanas or the Greeks mentioned as a warrior tribe, which has become Shūdra, by not consulting the Brāhmanas. Probability of their mention falls within the period 327 B. C. (the date of Alexander's invasion) to 350 A. D. Vish*n*u Purā*n*a testifies the existence of Yavanas along with Shakas as a warrior class, after the fall of the Andhras in the year 227 A. D. But in the year 350 A. D. in the inscription of Samudra

Gupta, we hear of Shakas and Pahlavas (the reference is regarding Shāhis and Shahānushāhis, whom I regard to be Pahlavas), but we do not hear of Yavanas. Shakas, Yavanas, and Pahlavas[3] are mentioned together by Gautamīputra in his inscriptions, as early as 113 A. D.; thus the period of the close association of the names of these foreigners falls within 113–350 A. D.

We now come to Lichchivis. The Gupta dynasty which prided itself on their descent from Lichchivi on the mother's side rose into importance in 320 A. D. After that date, to put down Lichchivi as a Vrātya tribe was not possible.

We want a period when all that our text wrote regarding Andhras, Shakas, Yavanas and Pahlavas was possible, and such a period cannot be any other than 227–320 A. D.[4]

The author's home.— This is not hard to determine. There is a good deal of evidence to show that the writer was a Brāhmana of Magadha. He manifests a good acquaintance with this region, and very little with

[3] A confusion hangs over the names Shaka and Pahlava Whether the dynasty of Western Satraps were Shakas or Pahlavas cannot be very definitely told; but this confusion need not disquiet us for the present. We know for certain all we care to know, that Shakas and Pahlavas existed in India for a long time, side by side, probably since 78 A. D., and the period of this close association falls between 113–350 A. D.

[4] Burnell's introduction to his translation contains an argument on the date and place of our text. The faulty character of these arguments is well shown by Hopkins in the foot-notes Hopkins has summed up and criticised the argument of Burnell again in PAOS., May, 1885. He concludes that Burnell brings us not one step nearer the solution of the problem. Hopkins has examined the discussion on the date by Bühler. He thinks Bühler's conclusions probable but not absolutely proven by the arguments given (PAOS, May, 1887).

others. Even a glance at the list of the castes he has given would be enough to convince us of this. Either from ignorance or some specific motive, he does not mention any caste or tribe in Southern India, except the Dravidas and Choda (who were too well known to be forgotten or slighted), though such castes or tribes were at least as numerous in the South as they were in the North. He treats of castes like Khasas and Karanas (quite insignificant in the history of the period), and even speaks of Lichchivis who were only a clan. There are castes like Mallas[5] mentioned herein, while castes of those names are found in Bengal; but it is uncertain whether they are the same.

He speaks of nationalities like Paundrakas and Udras[6] which are but people of two parts of Bengal, the former are identified with modern Pōds.

Many of the peoples whom he speaks of have not

[5] There was a clan called by the name of Mallas in the drama of The Little Clay Cart (Mrichchakatika) we find Shakara boasting of his descent from a great family like Mallas. We have many other references to this clan (Kula) in the Sanskrit literature. But our author evidently did not mean this clan, for he again speaks of Zalla, Mallas and Natas, as men who subsist by despicable occupations, and as men addicted to gambling and drinking (xii, 45). This reference plainly shows that Mallas were a tribe and not a clan. Mention of Mallas and Natas and Karanas together also is significant. All these three tribes are found in Bengal and have nearly the same status.

[6] In Jolly's critical edition he gives an important variation of reading for x, 44. Instead of Udras he gives Chodas and he does not make any mention of Khasas. But our author mentions Khasas elsewhere according to Jolly's text, and that too as a degraded tribe of Kshatriyas (x, 22). The mention of Chodas in the place of Udras does weaken the argument to a certain extent. At the same time the reading chosen by Jolly is not to be entirely relied upon. Out of nine manuscripts which he collated, only two give the reading he has given; while there are two which give Udras, and three give a reading nearer to Udras than to Chodas.

yet been identified with any present caste, *e. g.* Pukkasas, Ve*n*as, Chunchus.

Among the peoples he speaks of who were away from his district we find Medas, Avantyas, Vaidehakas, Daradas, but such tribes are too few. But if we consider the tribes near Magadha mentioned by him we have Nishadas, Kaivartas, Cha*nd*alas, Lichchivis, Pau*n*dras, Kara*n*as, Khasas, etc.

It is true that he makes a mention of Shakas, Yavanas, and Pahlavas who lived mainly in Western India, far from the place of the writer, but it must be remembered that they were foreign tribes, who were making their existence felt all over India. His mention of the Chinese is very significant; it is highly probable that many Chinese had visited the country as pilgrims since the introduction of Buddhism into China, and the conversion of the Chinese emperor to Buddhism in 67 A. D. The usual route of these pilgrims was along the side of the river Ganges. Those pilgrims who have left records and passed along this way are known to us. *i. e.* Fahien (399 A. D.) Hiouen Thsang (629) I-Tsing (671–695). On account of such pilgrims, the writer must have felt the necessity of laying down a rule, for guidance in the treatment of the representatives of the nation whom he well knew to be adherents of a heresy. He would have been perfectly willing to call these people Kshatriyas had they only paid homage to Brāhma*n*as.[7]

[7] We hear of Chīnas in Mahābhārata and in both northern and southern recensions of Rāmāya*n*a. But our object here is not to find out the date of contact or acquaintance of the two countries, but the probable reason of their mention by Mānava-dharma-shāstra.

For the proper comprehension of what I have just said, it is necessary to make a few comments on the knowledge which the Hindus had concerning other peoples. There did exist commercial relations between India on one hand and on the other the peoples of Western Asia and beyond (the Greeks and the Romans), Southern Asia (including Kambodia and Jáva) and with those of Northern, especially Northeastern Asia. But although the Pa*nd*yas might have been acquainted with the Javanese, and although the Shakas and people of Ceylon might have known the Romans, it does not follow that the people of Pā*t*aliputra were necessarily acquainted with them. Not only that, but the different peoples of the continent of India did not necessarily know each other, though one nation might know of their next-door neighbors and the latter again know or know of peoples dwelling further away.

This is not all. It was a strange irony of fate that the people who came forth as the expounders of dharma were persons who had the least knowledge of the world. The Brāhma*n*as with their ideals of purity remained aloof from the rest, and the difficulties in the transmission of knowledge from one layer of society to another were becoming greater and greater. These facts account for the nonmention in the caste-lists of many races of Southern India, of Romans, and of people of the islands in the Indian ocean, in a book which had for its object to explain the existence of all castes and to determine their status.

Let us now come to a rather vexing question as to whether we should draw any conclusion from the writer's treatment of the degree of sacredness of different spots in India. The land between the divine rivers Sarasvatī and Drishadvatī is according to him the holiest of all and is called Brahmāvarta. It is a land of the standard castes. The land of Kurus, Matsyas, Pāñchalas, Shūrasenakas ranks immediately after Brahmāvarta and the usages of the Brāhmaṇas of that place are standard and authoritative. He then speaks of Madhyadesha or the midland which contains all the land between Prayāga and the disappeared river Sarasvatī and between Vindhya and Himālaya, a territory which includes the countries just mentioned (JAOS, xix). He then proceeds to define the Aryāvarta, or the land of the āryas, as the land between Himālaya and Vindhya, extending as far as the eastern and the western oceans; the significance of this name of the territory being that it is a place fit for the performance of the sacrifices, and that all the twice-born should seek to dwell there. He adds (ii, 17–24) that the regions other than this are the country of the Mlechchas or barbarians, where only Shūdras distressed for subsistence may dwell.

Let us first realize what all this means.. First of all he draws a sharp line around the territory of Madhyadesha to separate it from all other territory, and also between the eastern and western divisions of it. It is true that he assigns a higher status to the inhabitants of the western part, but he deems the customs and usages of Brahmaṇas of the other part just as good or even better to be taken as a standard. He thus virtually sets up a doctrine that the regions throughout which the Brāhmaṇas may claim that their conduct, customs, and usages are standard are much more extensive than those throughout which the other castes can do so.

What we want to find out is the responsibility and the personal element in these doctrines, and therefore the traditional doctrines should be sharply separated from those of our author. Although we ought perhaps to hold an author responsible for the doctrines which he derives from others, and ought to base our conclusions regarding his personality upon them, nevertheless it would be safer to base our conclusions entirely on the innovations which the author has made. The only writers who allude to similar doctrines are Vasishtha and Baudhāyana. Vasishtha no doubt derides the validity of usages which are opposed to those of Aryāvarta, but he feels a doubt as to the exact limits of the region. Whether it is the country situated between Ganges and Jamna or the one between Sarasvati and Black-forest (Kāla-vana), or whether it is the entire Northern India as our author holds. He again does not condemn the Dekkhan as the land of the Mlechchas.

Baudhāyana as I interpret him gives two sides of the question. One school said that the customs and practices of the North are valid for the North, and those of the South are valid for the South; while others held that the consideration whether a certain conduct is customary in the South or North should be left aside and the question decided according as the practice is approved by men pure and learned in the Vedas. He further holds that the rule of conduct that prevails in Āryāvarta is authoritative; but he also expresses two opinions as to the extent of Aryāvarta. The conservative opinion regarded the small strip of land between the Ganges and Jamna as Āryāvarta, while others held it to be the land between the disappeared river Saraswati and Black forest, and between Himālaya and Vindhya.

The strong antipathy against the Dekkhan which we find in our text cannot be found in the earlier books.[8]

The doctrine that the Brāhmanas can claim for their conduct and usages standard authority over regions much greater than those throughout which other castes can do so cannot be traced in earlier books.

A corollary to the above recited doctrines is that a Brāhmana who was born in a country which is second best and lives anywhere in Āryāvarta should be looked up to, and that all the people should learn right conduct from him. This is something very significant in determining the location of the author.

Expression of so quaint an idea at the very beginning of the book appears like an unconscious apology on the part of a Brāhmana who may be living outside the central regions (Madhyadesha) for presuming to write a work on dharma.

The author's personal character.— The date and the place of our author being determined, we now turn to his personal character. If we read the book critically the author, with all his exaggerations and uncouth rules, does not impress us unfavorably. The author apparently was a very learned man of his period, who

[8] It is true that Baudhāyana prescribes a penance for those who would migrate to the country of the Kāraskāras which is a part of Dekkhan, but he prescribes it also even for those who lived in almost all parts of Northern India excepting Madhyadesha.

had studied dharma as taught by different schools, Vedas, various systems of philosophy, Upanishads, Kalpa literature, epics, rhetoric, and Purā*n*as. Though he borrows from other writers, he occasionally tries to find out a Vedic authority for various statements. His knowledge of various writers is well attested by his statements, which can be identified as virtual quotatations from certain books. His knowledge of the Purā*n*as (iii, 232) is also to be inferred from his references to Purā*n*as and Puranic characters, like Vena, Manu, Nahusha, Vishvāmitra, etc. What philosophy he believed in is a very hard question to settle. First of all the history of philosophy is not well worked out. Again, it appears that he carefully avoided committing himself to any doctrines of philosophy save those which were accepted by all. It is true that he believed in the doctrine of three Gu*n*as, which is essentially a Sānkhya doctrine, but inasmuch as this doctrine is discoverable in the Upanishads, and other schools do not oppose it, I am not inclined to call it a sectarian belief. Some of his theories like "From the union of water and fire arose the glittering gold and silver" (v, 113) are Vedic and belong to no special school. Vaisheshikas, for example, consider gold and fire to be of the same element—Tejas. Such a vague thesis is not to be argued about as if it were a philosophical tenet; it is only a popular belief of the period. He must have had some knowledge of astronomy and medicine. In his advice he tells what kind of wife should be selected. He also tells about the proper period for approaching the wife. In giving such precepts he explains the medical and astronomical reasons. He was well acquainted with the nīti literature. The relation of dharma and nīti will be discussed later.

Our author was more than learned, he was a man with good intentions. There are many passages in the text which appear to us ridiculous and unjust, but we need not condemn the author hastily for that reason, and should bear in mind that he was bound to respect the tradition. He mixes up his own sentiment quite often with the injunctions, and those sentiments indicate that he was a man kind-hearted,[9] paying more regard to virtue than to forms,[10] lover of moderation, and trying to be fair to other castes.[11]

More than this. We find him a progressive man. Thus there were various antiquated rules which were valid once, but which shock our present ideas of morality and equity. These he either contradicts or treats as restricted in their application,[12] or explains in some novel manner.

[9] See his treatment of theft, adultery, and treatment of other castes by the Brāhmaṇas.

[10] He says: "Neither the study of the Veda, nor liberality, nor any (self-imposed) restraint, ever bring rewards to a man whose heart is contaminated by sensuality."

[11] If one wishes to find out the moderation of our writer we should only compare his views on adultery and rape with those of Vasishṭha. Our writer prescribed death only in one extreme case, while Vasishṭha prescribes death at almost every imaginable place. Compare also the rules given by our author regarding the disposition of treasure-trove. Perhaps in the advocacy of moderation Buddhism had influence on him, or the age may have become more humane through the teaching of Buddha, and our author might have unconsciously caught the spirit of the age. He condemns for example the slaughter of animals, advises abstinence from meat of any kind. Even in the matter of sacrifices he regards slaughter as unnecessary.

[12] A good example is afforded by his treatment of the matter of the Levitical marriage or appointment of the brother-in-law to "raise up seed" to his deceased brother's widow, the Niyoga ix, 64-70.

About his personal views and tastes a good deal can be gathered from the book, but such a task would be unwise as it would lead us into details foreign to our purpose.[18]

---

[18] By the way I may say that there are two books in Burmese associated with the name of Manu:

1, *The Damathat or the laws of Menoo.* Translated from the Burmese by D. Richardson, Esq., xiv vols. complete in one. Burmese and English Maulmain. Burma. Amer. Baptist Mission Press, 1847. 8vo, pp. 752. This book starts with the story of creation, but involves Buddha in the story. Manu is depicted as a wise man, who would give decision on particular imaginary cases of law.

2. *King Waguru's Manu-dhammasatthana* text and translation. (Edited and translated by Emanuel Forchhammer, with a preface by John Jardine Rangoon, 1892.)

In this book there are various similarities. There are even some rules which we find in our text but do not find in the literature prior to it (like adulterous acts, vii, 358-359). But in the present condition of research it would be unsafe to make any conclusion.

In this book there is no ritual and the book comes very near what we may call positive law. But both the books are of very little use in our work.

CHAPTER V.

TREATMENT OF CASTE BY THE BOOK.

1. *Meaning of the Words.*

We now come to the subject-matter, the treatment of caste in Mānava dharma shāstra. Before giving the detailed precepts regarding different castes it is important to make every effort to understand the sense of the various terms which the writer used and which are supposed to have a bearing on caste.[a] We should also take notice of certain theories about caste which the writer believed in and without proper knowledge of which, his detailed instructions would be unintelligible. In particular we must understand the two words var*n*a and jāti. Our author emphatically says that there are only four var*n*as and there is no fifth var*n*a (x, 4)[1] while he admits over fifty jātis. Thus he uses var*n*a as a comprehensive term which included several jātis. Var*n*a according to him are four divisions into which these castes are grouped. But he often uses the word

[a] In this chapter and in several others, Western scholars are likely to think that I am answering some imaginary arguments. But I am not. On account of some unhappy mistakes by some Western scholars, and on account of their words passing as authority, a host of beliefs have sprung up in the minds of Indians educated in English, who often display a lack of judgment in their estimate of the work of European scholars. And these beliefs often find their expression in the vernacular literature or through the English newspapers conducted by educated Hindus, which have their influence on the masses.

[1] Our writer has misused the word var*n*a in one place. He speaks of fifteen var*n*a in x, 31, where he simply meant fifteen jātis. The commentators have noticed this incongruity and have given the readers the proper warning.

"jāti" in a very comprehensive sense. For example he calls Brāhmana a jāti, and Shūdra a jāti. Thus, though many jātis together form one varna, the whole varna may be a jāti. This use clearly shows the fact, that the use of the word "jāti" to denote both smaller and larger groups prevailed at the period of our writer as it prevails now, and I suppose that this confusion existed at a period still more remote.

But what did he mean by the word "jāti." Jāti means the form of existence as it is determined by birth. Use of the word "jāti" in a sense very similar to this belongs to a much older date and can be traced in Vedic literature. In Nyaya and Vaisheshika philosophy it developed the meaning of "species." In popular usage Brāhmana was a jāti, Chāndāla was a jāti, horse was a jāti, and man was a jāti.

Whether our writer used the word "varna" in that sense in which the Americans use the word "color," is a question which must be settled.[2] Our writer used the words "ārya varna" and Shūdra varna" and if we really wish to understand him and not misunderstand him we should try to translate these words, not with

[2] Great confusion has been created by vain analogies. White races came in contact with dark races in America as they did four thousand years ago in India, and attempts are made to discover the "color prejudice" in every document of this ancient land. Still more confusion is created by the various meanings which the word "ārya" acquired in India and which the word "Aryan" acquired in the Western World. The word "ārya" was never used in India in the sense of the word "race" (if we take the word "race" in its larger sense). The conception of race is a very modern one if it exists in any definite form at all. Ethnologists with all their labor do not yet know what the word really means, and if we interpret the Indian documents with modern or foreign ideas in our minds, the result will be a mischief to science and social institutions.

the Vedic vocabulary or with the semideveloped vocabulary of the modern ethnology, in our minds, but we should try to translate the words in the sense current at the time of our writer.[8]

Our writer never defined the term "ārya." The people for whom he wrote understood perfectly what "ārya" meant. What meaning he had in mind — the meaning which was accepted by the people of India for centuries before and after the period of our writer — must be gathered from the uses of the word "ārya" in the text.

[8] The discovery, or rather the invention (for this is what we ought to call it), of racial lines in the present varna system of Hindu society, made by European scholars on the basis of Vedic literature, deserves severe condemnation, not so much for their unhappy mistakes (which are certainly excusable), but for the consequences which they have produced in India. Europeans have told us that Aryans and Dravidians are two different races. The again tell us that races which are widely differentiated should not mix. The present Hindus of ordinary English education (which means very poor and distorted education) seek justification and maintenance of the caste-system in the application of those principles. Modern Hindus have contempt for Brahmanical rites and are thus separated from Brāhmana orthodoxy and Brāhmana ideas. The Brāhmana orthodoxy does not know what Aryan or Dravidian means, nor does it care to inquire into it for its purposes. All that the Brāhmanas care to inquire about is Sanskāra (the sacraments) and Karman (the aggregate of a man's action as determining his future fate-character), to which they attach very high value, but which they will perhaps give up with the growth of liberal sentiment.

But the Hindu of English education is quite different. Hearing of the conditions in the United States, those Hindus who think themselves to be Aryans, wish to demark themselves sharply from those whom they think to be Dravidians. Again, as a great mystery hangs over the consecrated word "Aryan," almost every caste thinks itself an Aryan caste and tries to remain aloof from the rest. I have noticed the black peoples of the Bengals, with clearly Mongoloid features, who would despise Dravidians (Tamils, for instance), who had developed

For centuries, till the arrival of European scholars on Indian soil, the people of India never meant by the word "ārya" that race of invaders who reduced the natives of the soil to servitude. The word indeed probably had such a meaning, but only for a short period antedating the concrete beginnings of civilization in India. Before the close of the period of the composition of the *Rig*-Veda the descendants of the invading tribes had forgotten where they came from, and thought themselves to be autochthonous and men of noble qualities

high civilization and literature and enjoyed high prestige in the peninsula long before the English people conquered Bengal, gave it a sort of uniformity and raised the people to some importance in the land. In India if there are any people who are very proud of their pure Aryan blood, it is the black Bengalese of Mongoloid features, and among them especially those who can claim their descent from the five Brāhma*n*as and five Kāyasthas who in fact were imported from the upper valley in order to improve the local breed according to the traditions of the Kulīna system. It is amusing to observe that some educated Bengalese are now, since the Russo-Japanese war, quite willing to admit their racial connection with the Mongolian stock.

These phenomena are not peculiar to the Bengals. Some Maratha Brāhma*n*as also try to maintain sharp separation from the rest because they are Aryans and the rest of the castes are Dravidians, and if they fuse it would be an unspeakable sacrilege and a disaster. Some other castes below them who call themselves Brāhma*n*as and are very virulent in their attacks against recognized Brāhma*n*as and talk of the principal of equality when their betters wish to exclude them, try to separate themselves just as sharply from the population below them, because the former are Aryans and the latter are Dravidians.

The Dravidians are in fact a fine race and have produced men and women of whom any one in the world may well be proud, and the proudest races need not be ashamed of alliance with them. I shall be very sorry, if a superficial acquaintance with a half-developed and hybrid ethnology, and a wrong interpretation of ancient documents, and an invented tradition, should result in magnifying racial differences and in making the future consolidation and amalgamation of India more difficult and distant.

and culture. The word "ārya" had received some sanctity, and had become rather a title to be applied to properly qualified people, than a word expressive of the recently-born conception of race. Occidental scholars, who usually attach more importance to the study of Vedas than to the later Sanskrit literature, revived the long-forgotten Vedic meaning of the word, and made it once more current, although since the beginning of India's characteristic civilization (say from the close of Rig Veda) until 1800 A. D. the word had a meaning entirely different.[4]

According to our writer, any man who is not Mlechcha, Dasyu, Vrātya, Vāhya, Shūdra, is an ārya. The word is used in the sense of honorable man (viii, 395). He contrasted ārya with Mlechcha. Mlechchas were barbarians whose country was other than the country of the āryas and who spoke language different from those which āryas spoke (ii, 22, 23; x, 45).[5]

Dasyus were persons who were neither Brāhma*n*as, Kshatriyas, Vaishyas, nor Shūdras (x, 45). Who these Dasyus were we do not know exactly. At v, 131, the term "dasyu" is applied to "Chā*nd*ālas and others."[6]

[4] I know of a case which occurred about ten years ago in the Maratha country, in which two young men, returning from England and Japan, submitted to a fine imposed on them by the Brahmins. The former was fined one hundred and fifty rupees because he went to a Mlechchha country, and the latter was fined one hundred and twenty rupees because he went to an ārya country, but crossed the sea, and did not observe proper ceremonial on the way.

[5] I do not think that the words of these passages mean languages of the Turanian or the Dravidian group. They cannot be so interpreted, unless we add a good deal of modern fancy to the statements of the original.

[6] I am of the opinion that at this time there was no such caste as Dasyus, but the word had become a classical term of

Vrātyas were persons of various castes, who did not undergo the sixteen ceremonies. Contemptuous treatment of Vrātya is seen in almost every chapter of the text. He forbids intermarriage with Vrātyas, speaks of the descendants of Vrātya as Shūdras, forbids sacrificing for Vrātyas, and prescribes the same penance for sexual intercourse with a Vrātya woman as he does for such relation with a Chā*nd*āla woman.

A Vāhya was a person excluded by the community This class probably differed very slightly from Vrātya in the treatment by dharma.

We come at last to the Shūdras. Our writer I think does not regard the Shūdras as ārya. There are many references which hint this idea indirectly, but he has never committed himself in any of the places. He has not contrasted ārya with Shūdra, but has on various occasions contrasted twice-born and Shūdra. But he has indirectly hinted that Shūdra is not ārya by declaring that every ārya must study Vedas (ii, 165). In the whole book there is not a single expression which would indicate that our writer has any conception of what we may call race, and the readers of our text should take every care not to put into the word "ārya" a meaning which modern philology has attached to the English word "Aryan." Had the Chinese only respected Brāhma*n*as our writer would have been perfectly willing to call them Kshatriyas and therefore āryas. People who may have been born in an Aryan family or tribe,

contempt (*e. g.*, viii, 66; x, 32; xi, 81; xii, 70). Dasyus are contrasted with āryas in the Vedas, and our writer, who was a Vedic scholar, would probably have regarded his book as incomplete unless he made use of such a term.

but had been excluded for improper conduct, ceased to be āryas. The question whether a person was Aryan or not had very little to do with his caste. Whatever relation there may have been between race and caste in the Rig Vedic period the race question was not of any significance in the period of our writer.

When in the times of our writer, a question arose as to whether a certain family was ārya or not, one did not ask whether this family could trace its connection with those invaders who came from the northwest, and slaughtered the natives of the soil by thousands, but only whether the family was descended from the people already regarded as ārya. The princes of the soil who held their own against the Aryan invaders were by no means excluded from the title "ārya." All the princes whether they belonged to the so-called Aryan race, or the so-called Dravidian race were āryas. Whether a tribe or a family was racially Aryan or Dravidian was a question which never troubled the people of India until foreign scholars came in and began to draw the line. The color of the skin had long ceased to be a matter of importance.[7]

[7] The attitude of the author of the Dharmashāstra in this regard is essentially that of the writers of the epic, to whom ārya was rather ethical than ethnic. Thus an ārya act was a noble act, whoever performed it, and an ārya was a gentleman. Naturally the slave caste as a whole were not representative gentlemen, though, theoretically, a good Shūdra might be so regarded, as a low-born man in the Western world might reluctantly be given the same title, if his virtue or heroism raised him above his caste level. The attitude toward strangers was also not unlike that of the insular Englishman toward foreigners. They were rather despised because they were foreigners, but it was not denied that some of them, by virtue of their bravery or skill, were noble or gentlemen (ārya). If they accepted the standard religion their status was unquestioned; otherwise

2. *Types of Castes*

I do not care to reproduce here the dry list of jātis (castes) which our writer has supplied to us. Many of the castes which may have been easily recognizable at the period of our author cannot be recognized now. The castes may have changed names, and some of them may even have ceased to exist. We are not again interested in any special caste here, but in the general growth of the system. We are interested in the causes which create social differences amounting to caste. The following kinds of castes are distinguished by our writer:

- i. Four original var*n*as.
- ii. Castes which were supposed to be produced by mixture with pure and mixed caste.
- iii. Castes which have lost their status on account of neglect of sacred rites.
- iv. Castes due to the exclusion of persons from the community.
- v. Slaves and their descendants.
- vi. Peoples excluded from the community of four var*n*as, as well as their descendants.

The question of the origin and development of the four var*n*as need not be entered upon here. I intend to give this question a very detailed and independent treatment in another work. Suffice it to say that our author has simply repeated the Vedic theory of the origin of four var*n*as from the mouth, arms, thighs, and feet of Purusha in a different form.

they were looked upon unfavorably, much as natives who were heretics were regarded, or, again, much as Englishmen of the last century regarded Dissenters.

He has given a long list of what he supposed to be mixed castes. These mixed castes, which are about thirty in number, resolve themselves into three types:

1. Caste produced from two different pure castes; 2. Those produced by the mixture of pure castes on one side and mixed on the other; 3. And those produced from parents of mixed origin on both sides.

Let us see the sources of the doctrines given to us by our writer. The writers before him who have discussed mixed castes are Baudhāyana, Vasish*t*ha, and Gautama. Vasish*t*ha and Gautama have spoken about the mixed castes produced by unequal marriages. Of such castes, Vasish*t*ha gives ten. Gautama gives two opinions; one opinion gives ten mixed castes while the other gives twelve.

The writer who gives "mixed castes" of all the three types stated above is Baudhāyana. Of the first type, *i. e.*, castes born of pure parents of different castes, he enumerates eleven. He names two low castes as born of parents, one of whom was pure, Shūdra, and the other was mixed; he also gives two castes where both parents were of mixed origin.

In our text the doctrines already enunciated by earlier writers appear to have been carried much further by our author. He has given nearly thirty of these mixed castes, which were arrived at by permutation and combination of those known before. It may also be observed that our writer did not take notice of certain castes enumerated by his predecessors. They are Rāmaka, Rathakara, Daushyanta, Mūrdhāvasikta, Ðhīvara and Māhishya. I intend to discuss elsewhere why the writers on castes felt the necessity of explaining the existence of new castes by the indiscriminate intermixture of two already existing, but I must say a few words regarding the authorship of such theories of this nature as were invented to explain away the origin of new castes.

When we find a writer making a statement regarding the origin of a new caste for the first time we should not make haste to draw a conclusion that the author is the inventor of the theory. The doctrine which he records he may derive either from another author or an authoritative teacher who may have transmitted his doctrines by oral instruction. It may also happen that a writer should receive such doctrines from popular beliefs. It is possible that a theory may be current among people but may never appear in any book. Again, the writer who may see the growth of such a theory may entirely ignore it, knowing the real facts about the matter. But later on the facts may be forgotten, and to a theory which one author may have received with distrust a later author may give some credence. For this reason, unless we have any positive evidence, we should not come to any hasty conclusion making an author responsible for the invention of wild theories which he may incorporate in his book; though we may safely regard him as guilty of recording the belief without examination.[8]

[8] The phenomena of springing up of new theories have not entirely disappeared from India yet. For the amusement of my readers, I may well record some theories, regarding the origin of some new nationalities or tribes which have made their appearance in the Maratha country, and which are still current among the folks there. I have heard of a theory of the origin of the Parsis from a Brāhmaṇa woman who married a man of

Let us now come to the castes of the third type, the Vrātyas, and their descendants. Vrātyas are those people who are born of twice-born castes marrying girls of equal caste, but have fallen in status as a consequence of neglecting the sacraments. Our writer has given more than a dozen castes as descendants of Vrātya-Brāhmaṇas or Vrātya-Kshatriyas or Vrātya-Vaishyas. He makes no mention of their status. There is an important passage in which he mentions that several Kshatriya

the Mahār caste, which is a large but untouchably low caste, in the Maratha country. The story was told to me in my boyhood. I have forgotten the details of the story, but it runs somewhat like this: A boy of the Mahār caste who was very fair and handsome attended a Vedic school, called himself a Brāhmaṇa boy. In fact his father was only a keeper of dogs. The boy was a very clever and diligent student and the teacher being very much pleased with him gave him his daughter in marriage. The ill-assorted couple had several children, but the children instead of being desirous of studying Vedas played with bones and showed their fondness for dogs. (No one can conceal his real nature; the real nature will be manifest some time!) The Brāhmaṇa's daughter, at once perceived the awkward and unbrahmanical tendencies of the boys, and suspected that her husband must have cheated her. She asked her husband about the matter and the husband confessed his guilt. The Brāhmaṇa woman, extremely agonized for being thus polluted, ascended the funeral pyre. While dying she cursed her husband, that his children would be hated in the land of the Bhāratas. They shall be treacherous, worshippers of the rising sun, flatterers, and liars. (I think I am correct in recalling all the malicious adjectives.) They will worship dogs, their corpses will receive no cremation, but be devoured by vultures. But inasmuch as these children were progeny of hers they will take to trade, but will never get the rank of Vaishyas, but will be regarded perpetually as Mlechchhas.

In the Maratha country there are still more fanciful theories about Englishmen, which need not be repeated here.

Alberūnī in his work on India speaks of the habit of telling a tale among the Pundits, when they do not have any satisfactory explanation. He has given the Indian theory of the causes of difference of dress and manners between Arabs and Hindus.

tribes have fallen to the condition of Shūdra by neglect of sacred rites and by disobedience to Brāhma*n*as. Of this kind he gives as examples the Pau*nd*rakas (the Pods), the U*d*ras (the people of Orissa), the Dravi*d*as (the people of Southern India), the Kambojas (Kabulis), the Yavanas (Bactrian Greeks), the Shakas (Scythians), the Pāradas, the Pahlavas (Persians), the Chīnas (Chinese), the Kirātas (Kirantis), the Daradas (Dards, a frontier tribe), and the Khasas (x, 43, 44).

It is much more difficult to understand a writer than to brush aside his passage as stupid and nonsensical, and cheap criticism has unnecessarily handled our author very roughly. To an historian of caste no other passage in the entire Sanskrit literature is so full of interest and meaning as the above. This passage explains why Hindu society could not assimilate the Mohammedans, when they had aready assimilated foreign peoples like Scythians and white Huns. It also explains why the Hindus intermarried with the Greeks of yore whom they called "Yavanas," but do not intermarry with the Englishmen now.

No other passage explains the attitude of the disciples of Brāhma*n*as toward other peoples on earth at a period when Buddhism was but a heresy, Christianity had not made its appearance in India, and the religion of Mohammed was yet to be born. These two verses may well be made the starting point when we wish to estimate the effect of the personal religions on the Hindu social system. It also supplies us with the key to the process of conversion to a religion which requires no baptism and attempts no conversion; it supplements the evidence to show the error of the doctrine that Hinduism does not admit foreigners to its fold.

One thing which a reader should notice is that in these verses the writer does not supply us with his doctrine regarding the origin of various castes mentioned above, but simply gives the reason why these various jātis fell to the position of Shūdras. Evidently he believed that Kshatriya var*n*a was composed of various jātis, and it really was. Some of these jātis maintained their status, while others lost it for the reason he has given us. How the different jātis or tribal castes originated, our writer does not pretend to explain.

He is simply recording phenomena which he observed in his days. The castes which adopted purer conduct and performed austerities raised their status in the eyes of the world, while the castes neglecting those elevating ceremonies and austerities fell. The writer never meant that these various tribes and nationalities, like the Chinese and the Greeks, were pieces fallen from one standard caste. He was well aware of the fact that there are various tribes in the world who rule and ought to be called Kshatriyas. He only explains why these warlike and ruling tribes are not considered as equals by the standard Kshatriyas of Kuru and Kosala. He never attempted to derive the entirety of mankind from the Indian population.

The Hindus of the period believed that the world is made up of various jātis and every one of these jātis belonged to one or the other of the four var*n*as. They never thought that the system of four var*n*as was peculiar to their own land.

Whenever Hindus and foreigners came into contact, if the foreigners accepted the religious ideas of the Hindus, the foreigners probably found no difficulty in entering Hindu society. If the foreigners did not accept the Hindu religious ideas they were treated as Mlechchhas. When the foreigners accepted the social and religious usages of the Hindus and thus found their way into the Hindu society, their jāti received the status which it could exact, as it always does. The Yavanas and Kirātas could not but be recognized as fighting tribes, but as they did not care to adopt all the ceremonial, they failed to get the status afterward which was connected with the ceremonial.

Whenever a family claimed to be of Kshatriya origir one of the easiest ways of determining the truth of such a claim was to find out whether Brāhma*n*as performed ceremonies in the family proper for a Kshatriya. This evidence was of a very high value because the conservative Brāhma*n*as went always by precedent. In the earlier days inducing Brāhma*n*a to perform such ceremonies was not difficult; but it became more and more difficult as time went on. Those who neglected the ceremonial once found it more difficult to establish it again. Thus the negligence of ceremonial on the part of Kirātas and Yavanas did them a perpetual harm by lowering their caste in the eyes of the public.

Formal conversion to Hinduism was unnecessary. They took it for granted that every man belonged to their religion, which is the only one and is eternal. The initiation or sacraments gave him only status. If a man neglected ceremonies or accepted heresies he fell.

3. *The constitution of the four varnas.*

Let us now inquire into the actual condition and constitution of the four var*n*as. The var*n*a Brāhma*n*a, the sacredotal class, whose traditional occupations were studying, teaching, receiving and bestowing gifts, etc., was by no means confined to those occupations; it was not possible for them to remain so. Our writer recognized this fact, as did some of his predecessors, and prescribed for them a number of occupations which a Brāhma*n*a might follow in time of distress. He also condemned as uninvitable to a Shrāddha those Brāhma*n*as who followed about thirty occupations[7] which were not proper for their var*n*a. This fact shows that the caste had taken a very wide latitude of occupation.

Again, these Brāhma*n*as were not an entirely democratic body amongst themselves, apart from the degradation that attached to the occupation followed. The Brāhma*n*a whose first wife was a Shūdra woman was himself looked down upon (iii, 155). Sons of adulteresses and widows were also considered as lowered (iii, 156, and see the rules regarding inheritances). Our author again thinks that children in order to be classed in the same var*n*a as that of the father should be begotten of wives wedded as virgins (x, 5). This appears to be

[7] The occupations which he thus condemned (iii, 151–166) were as follows: Teaching for money, selling of soma and flavors, bards, selling oils, keeping a gambling house and those of physicians and temple-priests and sellers of meat and shopkeepers, informers, messengers, architects, planters of trees, paid servant of the village, usurer, cattlemen, actors, singers, members of a corporation (ga*n*a), makers of bows and arrows, trainers of elephants, oxen, horses, camels, astrologers, bird fanciers, breeders of sporting dogs, falconers, farmers, shepherds, or keepers of buffalos.

one of the several steps by which Golaks ultimately became a caste. Besides these we have evidence that there were several pretenders who laid claim to being Brāhmanas, as there are now (viii, 20; vii, 85). The Brāhmanas called Vrātyas by our writer also must have been actually regarded as Brāhmanas by the public among whom they lived; but their claims to being Brāhmanas may only be denied by our writer and his sympathizers, just as the claim of the Brāhmanas of Bengal is sometimes denied to-day. The classification of Brāhmanas by locality, like Pancha-Gauda and Pancha-Dravida, does not appear to have arisen.

Our writer regards the son of a Brāhmana by a Kshatriya woman as a Brāhmana, but whether it was so or not is doubtful. From what I have said before regarding the nature of dharma it would not be difficult to estimate the value of our author's statement and to discover the facts at the basis of it. Our writer intended to refuse to recognize as valid the existing conditions when there was no Vedic authority. All that he meant by making the above remarks was that the son of a Kshatriya woman by a Brāhmana ought to be classed as a Brāhmana. The statement itself, unless supported by outside evidence, throws no light on the fact. The dubious way in which the writer has made the statement makes me feel very great doubt regarding the possibility of a Kshatriya woman's son being a Brāhmana. He writes (x, 6): "Sons begotten by twice-born men on wives of the next lower castes are declared to be similar to their fathers, but blamed on account of the fault inherent in their mothers."

A timid statement of this kind[8] reveals a doubt felt by the author in the matter, and such a doubt is very natural. Let us examine the causes which induced our writer to make such an indefinite statement. For this purpose a glimpse at certain other facts regarding the condition of the Brāhmaṇa caste becomes necessary. The Brāhmaṇas were not organized into a regular corporation which controlled the admission of persons to Brāhmaṇahood, but the recognition or nonrecognition of any person rested with individuals or groups who might have occasion to deal with him. For this reason the status of a man who pursued conduct that was supposed to be irregular was never definite. Some persons might admit a man of their company who committed an irregularity; others might not; and the same course must have been followed in the case of persons born of mixed marriages. Marriages of persons outside the varṇa must have been of comparatively rare occurrence. The princes, even those who would admit the superiority of a Brāhmaṇa, would hardly have cared to give their daughters to Brāhmaṇas excepting in cases where the Brāhmaṇas may have been landlords or high officers in the state. In the cases of sons by such marriages their claim to Brāhmaṇaship might have been admitted by some as it was denied by some. The main reason why our writer is inexact regarding the status of these sons is, in my opinion, the inexactness of the status itself.

[8] Timid because supported by "āhus" (they declare), yet it must be admitted that this distinction between "similar" and "co-equal" sons is said by the author to be "the ancient rule," and that the corresponding passages from Yājnavalkya I. 90 and Ushanas, cited by the commentator, show that the distinction was generally received.

This can be easily verified by paying attention to the various speculations regarding Ambashtha caste. The work of Baudhāyana holds that the sons of Brāhmanas by Kshatriya and Vaishya women, respectively, were Brāhmanas and Ambashthas. The works of Vasishtha and Gautama differ from it. The two latter works were separated from the former by nearly two hundred years,[9] but they are older than our text by about five hundred years. These two works give as their opinion that the Ambashthas are born of Brāhmanas by Kshatriya women. This kind of speculation involves in a way a denial to Brāhmanahood of the claim of the sons of Brāhmanas by Kshatriya women. Thus a blemish against such a son is of considerable antiquity, but our author does not like the idea of putting them into a different varna. I need hardly add that the Brāhmanas were at the top of society.[10]

Now let us turn to Kshatriyas. I have shown elsewhere that Kshatriyas never formed a caste. The royal families of several tribal kingdoms were doubtlessly

[9] I have relied on the estimates of George Bühler regarding the matter, and I think that he is probably correct.

[10] I do not care to open any discussion here, to contradict the statements of the students of Buddhism like Rhys Davids who hold that Kshatriyas stood at the top of society (Buddhist India, chap. iv). The times of which I am speaking are different from those which Rhys Davids has considered in his Buddhist India. At the same time, I confess that I do not think that Rhys Davids has proceeded properly in the treatment of the question. To him, Jātaka tales are superior, as historical documents, to the dharma works, to the works on nīti, and to the epics: He has given a discussion of social grades based on those tales. But the learned scholar has failed to give his reasons for such an attitude toward the various literatures. In my opinion there are several mistakes in his chapter on social grades. Of these I shall take notice at the proper place.

considered Kshatriyas, but also tribes which were dominant over one or more other tribes often arrogated to themselves the name of Kshatriya and had their claim allowed. Our writer has confused clans and tribes. There were clans or kindred families which dominated over the rest of the people of their own tribe, and there were some tribes which dominated over several tribes. Both of these classes were called Kshatriyas. The term Kshatriya was applied without regard to race or color. Any people who happened to be dominant called themselves Kshatriya and were accepted as such when they could exact homage. Kshatriyas were no close corporation. They were no organized body. Had the Moghals or the present Englishmen been without organized priesthood, and had they accepted the Brāhma*n*as as their spiritual guides and taken pains to adopt the elevating sacraments, they also could have formed one of the Kshatriya castes. These Kshatriyas had by no means drawn a sharp line between themselves and the masses as the Brāhma*n*as had done. How could they do so? Success in competition for the throne never depends on membership in a particular family. The man who rose, raised his whole family or tribe to Kshatriyahood; but when a tribe failed in strength, the whole tribe suffered in status. The history of the Kshatriya var*n*a with all its vicissitudes is a subject of very great complexity and interest and one which needs a special treatment.

I may state here that a wrong notion that Kshatriya was one united Indian jāti composed of royal families of Aryan race has done much toward the misconstruction of various ancient documents, and has led to the silly identification of Kshatriyas and Rajputs, and consequently the undue appreciation of the latter. This appreciation of Rajputs has led to the creation of pseudo Rajput castes and determined assertion on the part of Marathas of connection with and descent from Rajputs, though the Rajputs themselves were doubtless inferior to the Marathas in the vocations proper for a Kshatriya, namely, fighting and ruling.

What was the constitution of the Vaishya *varna*? Our writer has not given much direct information on this matter nor made allusions from which we could make helpful inferences. The occupations assigned to the Vaishya were to tend cattle, to trade, to lend money, and to cultivate land. He advises a Vaishya to follow up his business (vārtā) or to tend cattle (ix, 326) Here again he says that as long as a Vaishya is willing to keep cattle, cattle must not be kept by any other people. He advises him to learn the values of precious stones and metals and other commodities; to know different countries, profit and loss, scale of wages, languages, storing, purchase and sale. But it is significant that he does not advise a Vaishya to learn any of the trades like those of carpenter, shoemaker, barber, goldsmith, coppersmith, blacksmith, weaver, oil-presser, etc. It is very likely that all this was the work of Shūdras. He regarded all these as menial services. Some writers of bright imagination have conceived of a united Vaishya caste, a caste consisting of all people excepting Brāhma*n*as and Kshatriyas and low aboriginal castes, which, splitting itself, has produced the occupational castes of to-day. To justify this belief there is not a single reference in the text. Our writer classes all the castes whom he supposed to be born of intermixture as Shūdras, and this varna included castes which followed various professions, like those of physicians, charioteer (charioteer was regarded as very high in those times) and trades like those of carpenter (x, 47, 48), and even a caste which was engaged in commerce (the Magadhas). We must indeed admit that our author erred in deriving, as his predecessors did, the Ambasthas from two different parent tribes; but the fact that persons engaged in medicine and carpentry were regarded in his times and in his locality as base-born, is a fact which it would take a good deal of evidence to disprove.

Let us now find out how the Shūdra varna was constituted as it was conceived by our writer. I have already said that our writer carefully avoids making any statement as to whether a Shūdra was an ārya or not, though he has in many ways implied that Shūdra was not ārya.

The varna of Shūdra was by no means a caste or a group of castes composed of persons of the same status. Our writer and probably the Brāhmanas of his region included a number of castes and tribes in the varna Shūdra. They conceived that the low castes of their own region, as well as the ruling tribes which neglected the sacred rites and ceremonial, were Shūdras. Our author warns the Snātaka not to dwell in a country where Shūdras are rulers. This shows, however, that Shūdra kings actually existed, as we know from other sources, and as such they must have been recognized as Kshatriyas (rulers). The line of demarcation which separated Shūdras from the rest was not a matter of race, but was rather one of sacraments (Sanskāra). The term Shūdra was in process of changing its meaning.

But when our writer sets forth the duties of Shūdras he does not intend to prescribe the same duties for the ruling castes like Dravida and Paundra, but only for the low castes of his region.

Neglecting even these ruling tribes which were considered as Shūdras, the rest of the *varna* was by no means uniform in economic life. In the first place I must point out that it was not a slave caste, though the slaves were considered as Shūdras. It was mainly a class which was engaged in household service. The castes which followed occupations characteristic of inferior civilization, like basket-weaving and hunting, were also considered as Shūdras. There must have been some castes which tended cattle and were classed as Shūdras. Our writer permits handicrafts and trades which serve other castes as permissible to Shūdra, though for him domestic service in a Brāhmana's house was supposed to be most elevating.

Again, some Shūdras must have been rich people, for our writer says that a Vaishya and Shūdra shall pass through their misfortune on the strength of their wealth (xi, 34). Some Shūdras were also owners of slaves (ix, 179).

Regarding the accumulation of weath by a Shūdra our text writes: "No collection of wealth may be made by a Shūdra even though he be able to do it, for a Shūdra who has acquired wealth gives pain to Brāhmanas" (x, 129).

This is one of the verses which is an object of misinterpretation in various ways. This verse does not lay down any law which would prevent a Shūdra from accumulating wealth, but it only advises him for his own benefit that it is not a good thing for him to accumulate wealth if spiritual merit be his aim; or if he should become wealthy he is likely to be arrogant and disrespectful and would forget his duty of being humble, and he would thereby lose all his merit and a great obstacle would thus be thrown in the way of his ultimate elevation. This verse means nothing else. With all that the critics have written about the matter I am as yet unable to discover the rascality of the Brāhma*n*as in that verse, which really contains an admonition similar to that in the English prayer-book advising a poor man, "therewith to be contented;" that is, not to strive to raise himself above his station, as is expressly said in the preceding verse with a view to his future life as well as to this.

What, then, was the line between a Vaishya and a Shūdra? The main difference between them was that one was Dwija (twice-born) while the other was not. There was no such thing as a Vaishya caste which existed then and has now disappeared. Vaishya was a var*n*a and not a caste. The population consisted of various tribes then as it does now. These tribes differed in status then as they differ now. Some of these tribes or castes had gained the right of initiation while others had not. The question whether a certain person was a Vaishya or a Shūdra was decided, not by the actual condition of the man himself, but by that of the tribe or the caste to which he belonged. There were many tribes devoted to grazing cattle and agriculture; but these tribes were regarded as Vaishyas or Shūdras according as they possessed this sacrament or not. Those tribes which had received the right of Sanskāra were ārya tribes, while those which did not receive it were base-born. The economic distinction between Vaishya and Shūdra was not very sharp.

To sum up, let us see what all this means. All this gives us a picture of a society not much differing from the society of the present day. At the top of the social system were the Brāhma*n*as, and these Brāhma*n*as constituted not only a var*n*a but also a caste. Then came the Kshatriyas. These were not a definite united caste. The name Kshatriya was simply a collective one assumed by such castes and families as were then dominant. In like manner the Vaishyas. These were no caste. The name was merely a collective one comprehending the landed classes, cattle-keeping tribes, and clans of men engaged in commerce. The name Shūdra is applied as a collective one also to various castes engaged in commerce and skilled trades, unskilled labor and household service and other occupations held to be low. These last mentioned castes were regarded as low, chiefly for the reason that they were not entitled to the sacraments. Castes of one region were looked upon with suspicion by castes of other regions, and each regarded itself as superior to the others. The wild tribes and the castes of a filthy way of life were regarded as lower even than the Shūdras.

I here discuss incidentally the behavior toward each other of such castes as the Brāhma*n*as looked down upon and regarded as Shūdras. Did they accept their lot as Shūdras and become a democratic body? Far from it. In a hierarchical society the human mind becomes so degraded that even the lowest feel a very great pride on even a very slight superiority over their neighbors.[11] To-day in India a number of castes are called Shūdras by the Brāhmaṇas, but these castes are by no means on the same level. Among Shūdras themselves the various castes are very variously rated as high or low or intermediate. The lower castes try to adopt manners (āchāra) of the higher castes, and thus they would raise their heads above others and disown any sort of connection with their former brothers. Such phenomena are seen to-day and probably were seen in the time of our writer. Our writer has made mention of pretenders to a higher caste more than once and commended the imitation of higher castes very highly (x, 127). Again, it seems improbable that the tribes which followed occupations that are characteristic of low civilization, the races which may have been once dominant, the peoples engaged in more or less skilled occupations, and peoples differing from each other in cleanliness and

[11] In a way almost all countries have a hierarchical society, the hierarchical character becomes more pronounced when the questions of race and occupation become mixed.

This phenomenum is seen in the United States. The various groups of the people can be graded as follows: 1. The blue bloods; 2. The New Englanders; 3. The born gentile Americans; 4. The English and Scotch immigrants; 5. The Irish; 6. Gentile immigrants from other countries of Western Europe; 7. Dagoes (Italians); 8. The Jews; 9. The Mongolians; 10. Negroes. Whether the Jews are above or below the Dagoes differs according to the locality.

In this country I have noticed the Irish thinking themselves quite superior to the Dutchman. The Chinese think themselves infinitely superior to the Negroes.

Though the Americans generally do not make much distinction between the Chinese and the Japanese, regarding them equally low, still I found some Japanese complaining very bitterly that some people call themselves Japanese in this country though they are only Chinese!

civilization and prestige would fraternize freely simply because they all have received no sacraments. We may or may not find references to such phenomena in the literature of the period, but a society with doctrines of purity and pollution so monstrously developed (as it will be shown in the next chapter) and so highly specialized as it is to-day could hardly be imagined without a process so closely allied with the doctrine.

4. The occupational castes.

Let us now venture to inquire whether occupational castes existed in the third century.[12] Before answering this question in the affirmative or negative we should be sure that we understand what are meant by occupational castes. Not finding the names of goldsmith, tailor, oil-man, barber, and blacksmith among the castes mentioned in the text, one is very likely hastily to conclude that occupational castes did not exist; that the Vaishya caste existed as a whole body, and that from this united caste the occupational castes split up later. Such conclusions are due simply to carelessness in interpreting our author. Scholars who hold them make no attempt to find out how the various occupational castes did develop or could develop nor to ascertain whether guilds only degenerated into castes or there were any other influences working in the land which ultimately developed the occupational castes.

We may define an occupational caste either as a caste the bulk of the people of which regard a particular oc-

[12] I intend to make the growth of occupational caste a special field of inquiry, but here I make only such remarks as bear on the question in hand.

cupation as their peculiar one, or as an aggregate of people who have by some means become associated with a certain occupation. With this definition such occupational castes are common in many communities. In many societies there is a tendency of division of occupations on racial lines — so much so that a peculiar occupation becomes associated with a peculiar tribe.[13] Thus in India an aggregate may be formed first and it may take to a peculiar trade afterward.

In India peoples of higher civilization were migrating eastward and coming into contact with those who were less civilized, and some sort of division of occupation in racial lines was taking place. All the occu-

[13] In America we find numerous cases of this kind. The fact that the Chinese are a caste of laundrymen is something every American knows. There are also occupational castes of Negro porters and of Japanese butlers. In many cities we find Italians and Greeks in the occupation of shoe blacking. In two or three cities I noticed that buying and selling second-hand clothes and shoes was a trade which was monopolized by or relegated to Russian Jews. Buying watches and jewelry or loaning money on them is also a trade of this tribe. In fashionable circles it has become customary to employ French nurses, and in some cities domestic service is the occupation of Irish girls. It is also considered a fashion to have a Negro waiter, so much so that the Negroes have begun to feel that to wait on tables is their peculiar occupation and privilege. Strangely enough in the eastern part of America the native of India has become associated with palmistry, astrology, fortune telling and jugglery, so much so that it pays a man to pass for a Hindu when he is not. I have heard of Spaniards in this profession advertising themselves as Hindu astrologers and palmists.

There are various causes which bring about such a condition. Ability to do no other work but some peculiar work, and willingness to work for less, on the part of certain tribes, contribute to this phenomena. It may somewhat be a result of fashion. Preponderance of fellow countrymen, in a particular trade becomes of great help to the new-comer. All these circumstances have their effect in dividing occupations on racial lines.

pational castes that we find to-day are not merely guilds converted into castes. In the case of many castes there is not even any tradition of guilds. The process of division of occupations on tribal or caste lines has not yet entirely ended. A strong tribal feeling already existing very often leads to the appropriation of a certain trade by a certain tribe.

We have plain and unmistakable statements in our text to that effect, which some scholars have taken care to ignore.[14]

The Sairandhra is described as a person who is skilled in adorning and attending his master. He, though not a slave, lives like a slave, and subsists by snaring animals.[14a]

The Maitreyaka is described as sweet-voiced, as ringing a bell at the appearance of dawn, and as continuously praising great men.

The Mārgava or Dasa is described as a person who subsists by working as a boatman and whom the inhabitants of Aryāvarta call Kaivarta.[15]

The Kārāvāra is described as a worker in leather.

The Pā*nd*usopka is described as a dealer in cane.

The Antyavasayī is described as a person who is em-

[14] It is a pity that even men of scholarship, in order to support the thesis that caste is a bad thing, should think it necessary to show that it did not exist formerly, and for this purpose be blind to plain evidence.

[14a] Compare this statement with the fact that Draupadī had called herself ts Sairandhrī, when she attended the queen of Matsyas, during her year of disguise (Ajñātavāsa).

[15] Even to-day there is a tribe in Bengal called Kaibartas, who regard navigation by boats as their traditional occupation.

ployed in burial grounds and despised even by those excluded (from ârya community)[16] (x, 32-39).

Farther on our text says:

"To the Sūtas (belong) the management of horses and chariots; to the Ambashthas, the art of healing; to the Vaidehakas, the service of women; to the Magadhas, trade."[17]

"Killing fish to the Nishādas, carpenters' work to the Āyogava, to the Medas, the Andhras, the Chunchus and the Madgus the slaughter of wild animals."

"To Kshattris, Ugras, Pukkasas, catching and killing of (animals) living in holes; to Dhigvanas working in leather, to Venas, beating the drum."

"Near well-known trees and burial grounds, on mountains and in groves let these (tribes) dwell, known (by certain marks) and subsisting by their peculiar occupations."

"But dwellings of the Chandalas and the Shvapākas shall be outside the village. They must be made Apapâtras[17a] and their wealth shall be dogs and donkeys."

"Their dress shall be the garments of the dead. They shall eat their food from broken dishes, black iron shall be their ornaments, and they must always wander from place to place (x, 47-52)."

[16] In Kādambari Pundarika (during his birth as a parrot, when he was caught by a Chandâla) regretted the fact that he had to enter the habitation of Chandâlas or Mātangas which were avoided even by foreigners (Mlechchas).

[17] In almost every drama we find a sūta employed to drive a chariot.

[17a] Apapâtra means a person so impure that even his touch would render a vessel impure, and therefore the vessels which such a person uses should be destroyed, and should never be used by an ârya. See page 24.

What does all this mean to an historical critic? Would a critic be justified in declaring that the occupations mentioned herein as peculiar to certain jātis are entirely an invention by the author, without any ground for it? Certainly not. We can find enough evidence to show that the various jātis were engaged in peculiar occupations just mentioned. It is not difficult to see that engaging in these various occupations by the said jātis must have been a fact well known in the period which our author wanted to explain. One critic ridicules our author by showing that the occupations mentioned herein did exist long before the date of our text, but this evidence does not in any way conflict with the statements of our text so as to impair their value. Our writer never meant that any of the castes named above came into existence to engage in a certain occupation. He has noticed, for example, various castes who had hunting for their occupation, and has noticed two castes as people who had working in leather for their occupation.

The fancifulness of the origin of various castes which our writer has given is a fact beyond dispute, but we need not, for that reason, be blind to the truth involved in the statement, though such a blindness may help us to form and maintain a very pleasing theory which lays at the door of Mohammedan conquest all the sin of splitting up the whole "Vaishya caste," which caste, as I have shown, is nothing but a creation of fancy.

Whether the guilds were degraded into castes at this period is a question which I regard as unsettled.

5. *Possibility of Changing One's Caste.*

Was there any possibility of changing from one caste into another, in the times under consideration? I think not. There is one reference to Vishvāmitra becoming a Brāhma*n*a owing to his humility (vii, 42), but here the writer is speaking of times long gone by and we have no reason to infer that he meant that a person could become a Brāhma*n*a in his days by adopting good conduct. This idea is entirely foreign to our text. Again, this verse is included in the treatment of duties of Kshatriya and the object is to point out to the kings the great importance of their being humble (toward priests) and courteous, and to show how things recognized as most difficult to be accomplished can be accomplished through modest demeanor. Our text again says (x, 41) that through the power of austerities or by or through the power of descent (the seed) the people obtain more exalted or lower rank among men in successive generations. In this passage the author makes a statement that the people can raise their status by austerities. This is no doubt true. That a caste, or a group of men in a certain caste, may receive sacraments, and adopt purer conduct, and thus raise their status, is a phenomenon which he is recording, and is true even of to-day, but whether a person could go from one caste into another is something not known. It may not be impossible that a tribal chief, calling himself a Kshatriya and succeeding in inducing Brāhma*n*as to confer on him the sacraments, may even marry with another person of Kshatriya var*n*a. But I have shown that Kshatriya was not a caste at this period and that it probably never was. There is no statement in the text which would give us any ground to infer that a person who was not born a Brāhmana could become one by austerities, or by any other method.[18] It is significant that our writer has given us many examples of lowering one's status, but he has not given examples of a caste raising it. There is only one reference to a raising of caste: if a Shūdra female marries a man of the highest caste, and if then the female offspring again marries a man of the highest caste, and so on for seven generations, then the children would obtain Brāhmanahood (x, 64).

To take this statement very seriously would lead us into an error. We may admit that the rule was valid enough during the period. Whether valid or not makes no difference. The conditions of the rule are such that no actual case of it may fairly be supposed ever to have occurred. In short, the rule sets up what are practically impossible conditions. Even now this rule is supposed to hold good. But do any cases like this ever happen? Does any body of people keep record of such cases? The writers of the olden times were always limited in their means of observation, and society was still more indiscriminate. This rule does not imply things as they were, but as they ought to have been. The progeny of indiscriminate marriages may either form a caste of itself or may smuggle itself into a higher caste, as soon

[18] Here it is necessary to remind the reader that as there were pretenders to Kshatriyahood, there were pretenders to Brāhmanahood. By making pretenses to Brāhmanahood people no doubt gain some status, though they may have no chance of mixing with standard Brāhmanas, as the latter would never acknowledge such pretensions.

as possible, or it may be content with a *varna* of lower standing. We see such facts now and we have no reason to suppose that they were any different at the times of our writer.[19]

To-day a person cannot go into a higher caste, but may fall from a high station, or a person may lose his caste and may mingle in disappointment among lower castes, which are not very particular about the matter. These phenomena probably existed in the period under consideration. I have already given the quotation where a list of Kshatriya castes are spoken of having suffered in status by not consulting Brāhma*n*a.

People belonging to the category of those who suffered in status were of different varieties. There were those who fell on account of their mixing with low castes or of neglect of sacred rites. There were also

[19] The conditions in the United States supply us with a parallel. There are laws in Southern and Western States preventing marriages between whites and other races. The laws define that a person who has one-eighth or more colored blood in him is a colored person and may not marry with a white person. This is a positive statute and not moral law (dharma). But facts are entirely different from those stated in the law; the mulattoes try to smuggle themselves into white society as soon as they can, and in many cases they do so successfully, before they have more than seven-eighths of white blood in them. (Some negro students in Cornell and Harvard Universities told me that they know several cases of young beautiful mulatto women marrying white men without revealing to them their real composition). The sentiment in the white community is extremely strong against marrying with persons who have one drop of negro blood in them. Though law would permit a white man to marry a negro woman who had less than one-eighth of negro blood, a white man of respectability would not marry a woman who has any at all. *The important fact is that the prevention of mixed marriage depends not on the degree of previous intermixture, but on the knowledge or ignorance of the blemish.*

the Vahyas and the Dasyus. The minute differences among the last two were more historical than practical and I do not care to dwell upon them here. One of the great causes why peoples often suffered in their status was their continued adhesion to Buddhism.

There were definite rules regarding excommunication, and there was a class of sins recognized as jātibhransha, *i. e.*, the sins which ought to cause loss of caste. They were giving pain to a Brāhma*n*a, smelling at things that ought not to be smelt,[20] smelling spirituous liquor, cheating, and unnatural offense against man (xi, 68).

There were also a class of sins like killing a donkey which would reduce a person to a condition of mixed caste (xi, 69). The rule giving the sins which reduce a man to the condition of mixed caste is very hard to interpret historically. The interpretation is rendered much more difficult as we do not know the source from which our writer has derived his doctrine. No ancient writer has referred to it.

Suppose there is a case of a man who has committed a sin which degrades a man to a mixed caste, and he did not care to take any penance. A question arises whether a man who is rejected by his caste-fellows would be taken in by another so-called "mixed caste" like Ambastha, Magadha, or Vaideha, which were in

[20] Here is again an evidence to show that the book is likely to be written near Bengal. We do not hear of any people losing caste on account of smelling things that ought not to be smelt in any other part of India except Bengal. In Bengal we have a tradition that the Tagores lost caste because their ancestors smelt food prpared by a Mohammedan. It should again be noted that this verse is the writer's own addition.

fact different nationalities or tribes having pride and dignity. Such an acceptance hardly seems possible. To-day, if a Brāhma*n*a is outcasted by his own caste-fellows, a caste which is lower in rank like Kayastha (clerk) or Sonar (goldsmith) will by no means receive him into its fold, at least in Mahārāsh*t*ra. This verse may mean if such a man is outcasted, he will marry any woman he can get of whatever caste she may be; and in that way he might beget a mixed progeny. But such would be the condition of those who would do the sins which cause loss of caste. I think this verse may simply be interpreted as a complement of the preceding verse and means nothing more than that the sins, like killing a horse, a donkey, a camel, or a deer, are sins which ought to degrade a man from his caste; but they are not so grave as those enumerated in the preceding verse, and they require less penance than those in the preceding verse.

CHAPTER VI.

PHILOSOPHY OF CASTE (VARNA ORDER).

1. *The Philosophical Theories.*

In order to understand the spirit of the ages which upheld caste and varna, one must take pains to understand the philosophy which justified this system. For without proper comprehension of the philosophy we shall unjustly condemn people for doctrines which appear to our eye as unjust, cruel, and monstrous. The philosophy may be wrong, it may have vitiated the ideas of people regarding justice and charity; but the devout people of those ages were not wanting in ideas of those virtues. They thought that they were doing only right by observing and maintaining the rules of four varnas and four āshramas.

Our writer believed that four varnas are created, and to each varna a proper duty is assigned to prevent social dissolution (i, 87). He also believed that dharma for every individual is determined by his origin, because the nature of every person is originally determined.[1]

[1] One reason why they believed in a doctrine like this is that the word "dharma" had various senses in which it was used, and the different ideas carried by the word were not clearly differentiated. "Dharma" meant nature also. It was also believed that every being is endowed with a certain nature at the primary creation which could not be changed. Whatever deeds people do, those they do according to their dharma or swabhāva, which was originally assigned to them by the Creator or Manu. They for example believed that Manu allotted to women love of their bed, of seat, of ornament, passions, wrath, malice, and bad conduct (ix, 17). The qualities determined their dhārma. Servitude is innate in Shūdra. It is a part of his

"But to whatever course of action the Lord at first appointed each (kind of beings), that alone it has spontaneously adopted in each succeeding creation."

"Whatever he assigned to each at the first creation, noxiousness or harmlessness, gentleness or ferocity, virtue or sin, truth or falsehood, that clung (afterward) spontaneously to it," (i, 28–29).

Our writer probably did not know what great disaster would follow if the fusion of varnas should take place, but he knew that some great disaster would follow.[2] Probably the fusion of varnas itself began to be looked upon as a great disaster. He had knowledge of a legend

nature (viii, 414), which nobody could take away from him, and this is the reason why servitude is his duty.

These ideas have not entirely disappeared to-day. When the present ruler of one Maratha state was chosen for Gadi (the throne), he was chosen for adoption on the principle of innate royalty among the different little boys who were the candidates. Some holes were made in the trousers of different boys without their knowledge. When the boys noticed the holes, all of them, excepting one, wanted their trousers repaired, while the boy who was the exception wanted a new pair of trousers. Thus he displayed his innate kingly quality.

[2] Some idea regarding the probable dangers of varna intermixture may be gathered from the treatment of adulterers in the text and from what Arjuna said to Krishna (Bhagavdgītā, chap. i).

"In consequence of the predominance of impiety, O Krishna, the women of the family become corrupt O, descendant of Vrishni, intermingling of Varnas results; that intermingling necessarily leads the family and the destroyers of family to hell; for when the ceremonies of offering the cakes of food and water (to them) fail, their ancestors fall to hell."

Compare with this the objection of Aristotle to communal marriage as advocated by Plato. It was this: Unholy acts done against fathers and mothers are more likely to be committed if the relationship is unknown and who would make atonement for them (Aristotle's Politics, ii,, c. 4).

of a period when confusion of castes took place (ix, 67), but probably did not have any idea of such a condition. To see Brāhmaṇas and Shudras mixed was something the very thought of which they abhorred.

The dharma writers wanted order in the society. If people who are meant for servitude be allowed to give it up, then there would be no servants left, and who then would perform their functions? Shūdras will begin to rule, who are unfit to rule, and this social order would be completely destroyed. They quite thoroughly believed that castes and varṇa are natural things associated invariably with specific qualities. A Shūdra cannot be of noble quality; servitude is his nature. If there be any doubt regarding the varṇa of any individual it would at once be revealed by his nature or by actions which are due to his nature (x, 57).

But a question will be asked, "Why is it that one man should be compelled to be a servant all his life, and another man be a Brāhmaṇa all his life, simply because his father was a servant or a Brahmaṇa? This is sheer injustice."

Our writer would say "No!" for he firmly believed in the theory of Karma, three guṇas, and transmigration of soul. All these three theories, as they applied them, justified the entire system. In the concluding chapter our author has given all those theories. There he says to the following effect:

By Karma (action) are caused the various conditions of men, the highest, the middling, and the lowest. In consequence of many sinful acts committed by one's body, voice, or mind, that individual in the next birth will become a bird, or a beast, or a low caste person respectively. There are three guṇas[3] (qualities), satva (goodness), rajas (activity), and tamas (darkness). When one of these three qualities predominates, the body becomes distinguished by that quality. The study of Vedas, austerity, and knowledge, and purity, etc., are marks of the quality of goodness. Delighting in adventure, want of firmness, indulgence in sexual pleasure are marks of the quality of activity. Cruelty, covetousness, evil life, etc., are marks of dark quality.

Through each of these qualities man obtains various transmigrations. It is preponderance of various qualities that determines the birth of man as a Brāhmaṇa or a Shūdra. Those who commit sins go into inferior existences or wombs; those who do good actions pass into superior wombs; and those who lead an ideal life obtain cessation of birth and death.[4]

Thus it will be noticed that Hindus of that period who upheld caste did not do so out of disregard for justice, but only out of regard for it. They held that the varṇa order is ordained for justice and human betterment. The mere statement of their belief in this matter sounds like a satire to a person who is unacquainted with their system of thought. They did not hold that a man should not have a chance to better his condition. They only

[3] I have translated the word "guṇa" by quality for the sake of convenience. In fact the Sānkhya philosophy which used these terms does not regard them as qualities merely, but regards guṇas as substances. "Goodness" and "darkness" were something like substances which dwelt in various objects.

[4] I have avoided here to explain how the doctrines of Heaven and Hell and Transmigration of Soul were reconciled, as this explanation is not necessary for our purposes.

denied him such a chance in that particular life which is after all a small portion of the entire human existence. To a Shūdra they gave distinct grounds to hope for a better life and an inducement to better his condition. For our text says: "A Shūdra who is pure, the servant of his betters, gentle in his speech, and free from pride, always seeks a refuge with Brāhmanas and attains in his next life a higher caste" (ix, 335).[5]

[5] It should not be considered that a hope of this kind is no hope at all. Such an assertion would show the ignorance of the capability of the human mind. I know for certain that such ideas and hopes regarding happiness in the next birth cheer the mind and control it. In the Toy-Cart (Mrichchkarika, act viii), Shakāra, the king's brother-in-law, asked his slave to kill the damsel Vasantasenā. The slave refused the order flatly in the following words:

"Beat me if you will. Kill me if you will. I cannot do what ought not to be done. Fate has already punished me with servitude, for the misdeeds of a former life, and I will not incur the penalty of being born again a slave."

I once met a Mahāra, who, fearing that I was going near him and that my purity might then be defiled in case I touched him, and that he might incur the sin of defiling my purity, cried out at once and made his caste known to me. I got into conversation with him. I found that Mahar, though illiterate, could repeat many verses of Tukaram, Namdeo and Chokhamela. He appeared to be well acquainted with the theories of Karma and Bhakti, and of transmigration of soul. He believed that though he was a Mahar in that birth, by some misdoings in his past life, he was going to become a Brāhmana in the next birth, as he felt the desire for learning Sanskrit, and reading Gītā and Purānas. He conceived that these desires were clear indications of the better birth which he was going to get in his next life.

I do not know how far such sentiments exist in other members of the tribe. But it is not improbable that very many of the low castes believe, or are made to believe, that they justly suffer in this condition as a retribution for the sins which they did in the past life.

How much better it would have been for the whites in the United States, had they taught the negroes the doctrines of Transmigration of Soul and Karma instead of Christianity!

2. *The Theory of Purity.*

The caste system was supported not only by theological doctrines like Karma and the Transmigration of Soul, but also by ideas like those regarding purity and pollution which had a practical bearing on life. The precedence of caste is always manifested by ideas of purity and pollution, and for this reason the ideas of the period as they are reflected in our text deserve careful examination.

Our work reveals the ideas on this subject in its various relations. The articles of food were divided into pure and impure by degrees. The various sections of the country differed greatly in sacredness and impurity. A principle that actions that are holy and sacred ought not to be done with impure associations appears to have been well recognized. Purifying agencies and ceremonies for purification existed. Purity was closely associated with good omen, *i. e.*, Those things which were pure were supposed to bring good result or fortune, by their association, as good omens do, and impure things would bring misery. Various substances were graded on the principle of purity. But how far the various castes were graded is less clear.

The most conspicuous field in which the Hindu notions regarding purity and pollution manifest themselves is their treatment of the important question of food.[5a] In order to determine whether anything is eatable or not the first question to be answered is, How

[5a] I have not given here reference to every statement, because those who care to look it up in the original can easily do so with the help of the index attached to the translation of our text by Dr. Bühler.

is the food obtained? The food obtained by begging was not considered impure food; but there also were various restrictions, under which alone a Brāhmana considered it eatable. They would inquire, Who is the giver of the food? Here not only the ideas of morality came into play but also the ideas of ceremonial purity. The food given by a thief, a prostitute, a cruel man, a liar, or a criminal was prohibited side by side with the food given by a musician, physician, hunter, by men of Ugra, Nishāda and Shūdra castes, by goldsmiths, stage players, dealers in weapons, basket-makers, washermen, dyers, carpenters, and money-lenders. A supposition seems to have prevailed that a person's intelligence and desires will be like those of the man whose food he has eaten, and it was also supposed that the people engaged in the occupations mentioned above were not quite moral people.

The restrictions did not end here. The food, even if it be given by a proper person, may not necessarily be eatable. It may be rendered impure or it may be polluted. Impure food is intrinsically not pure, while polluted food is intrinsically pure, but considered impure by the people out of prejudice. Food that has turned sour, stale food, leavings of another person, food in which hair or insects are found, which had been pecked at by birds, on which anybody has sneezed, may be considered as impure food; food may be considered polluted when it is touched with the foot intentionally by anybody, or touched by a menstruating woman or by dogs. Our text does not distinguish between these two ideas of impurity and pollution, but classes both of them together.

Of these rules regarding food the most important were those which explained what substances should be consumed and what not. There were various rules regarding the use of meat, although it was considered meritorious to abstain from meat altogether. Again, a distinction was drawn between the food for Shūdra and that for twice-born. The twice-born, whose code of conduct was stricter than that of a Shūdra, was forbidden the use of a good many kinds of meat, like pork and chicken, and of vegetables, like onions, garlic, and mushrooms. Again, some sort of distinction was drawn between Brāhmana and the rest of the twice-born.

Penances also were prescribed to free a person from the guilt of eating food that he ought not to have eaten.

Some places were considered more sacred than others, while some were actually considered foul and polluting. The summary of the opinions of our writer has already been given where his locality is discussed. The writer is silent regarding the necessity of expiation for migrating into countries like Anga, Vanga, Kalinga, Sauvīra, and Deccan, while his predecessor, Baudhāyana insists on it. This fact, as I have said, shows greater liberality of the age regarding migration, or may probably hint something regarding the locality of the writer himself. There is one reference to show that falsely denying a Brāhmana's claim to nativity of his particular country[5b] was

[5b] This is I suspect to be an evidence for the locality of the author. The importance of the country of a Brāhmana is greater in Bengal than anywhere else. Though the Brāhmanas of Brahmavarta claim superiority over Brāhmanas of other parts, this superiority appears to be acknowledged in Bengal only; so much so that many Brāhmana tribes which have settled in Bengal for centuries would refuse to be called natives of province.

regarded as an offense somewhat like defamation, punishable with fine (viii, 273). But besides this there is not much in our text where purity or impurity of the country is made a matter of any consequence. The writer had a good opportunity to do so had he wished. He could have said that Dravidas, Shakas, etc., lost their status as a Kshatriya because they lived in Deccan.

Let us now find out if there was anything else to which purity or impurity was supposed to be attached. The part of the body above the navel was considered pure and the part below it was considered impure. Some animals were pure, while others were impure. Those which were impure were not only not fit to be eaten, but even their touch or look would make other things impure. Death or birth in the family would make the relatives and associates impure; and a long, elaborate code of rules existed which governed these matters. A menstruating woman was extremely impure; her touch, her look, and her voice carried pollution along with it.

Side by side with impure articles there existed two other kinds of articles, which may be called pure and purifying. Pure are those which are somewhat sacred in themselves but which would be polluted by associating with impure. Purifying are those which could not be polluted themselves and had the capacity of purifying others which may have been polluted. Also there were some things which could never be polluted, although they had no capacity for purifying others.

Pure actions ought not to be done with impure associations. For example, the study of Veda should not be done on any evil day or during the days of impurity due to the death or birth of a relative; nor should it be done in the presence of a Shūdra or a menstruating woman, or in impure places.

When it is said that some things are impure it should not be considered that all the impure things are equally impure. Things which a Snātaka may regard as impure other Brāhmanas may not so regard. Again, one impure thing would be polluted by contact with things more impure; *e. g.*, a Shūdra, who is more impure than a Brāhmana's corpse, may not carry it, though the corpse is an impure thing.

The purifying agencies were control of mind, austerities, fire, holy food, water, earth, the wind, the sacred rites, the sun, liberality, sacred text, etc. These agencies would purify from pollution or impurity, as the case may be. Our writer has given methods of purifying various inanimate things, like vessels made of gold, silver, and copper.

The purity or pollution of a Brāhmana was much more than what we may call physical purity and impurity. We may distinguish contamination or pollution from physical impurity, but our writer did not care to differentiate them sharply. If a Shūdra touches the food of a Brāhmana the Brāhmana feels that by some occult process the whole food has been spoiled and is rendered impure. Such food if eaten would make his body impure, at least just as much as food mixed with dirt or with articles that ought not to be eaten would do. All such ideas we can trace in the author before us.[6]

[6] The Brāhmanas have very strong ideas regarding the purity of their blood, which scarcely have a parallel anywhere else. Their purity of blood is not the same idea which ethnologists understand by these words. The racial purity is only a part of

The theory of purity and pollution will remain incomplete unless mention is made of the sacraments which held such an important place in the system. These sacraments were about sixteen ceremonies, from the conception of a man in his mother's womb until after the end of his life. These sacraments sanctify the body and purify from sin a person in this life and after death (ii, 27). By the Maunjī bandhana ceremony the taint derived from both parents is removed. By great sacrifices and Shrauta rites the human body is made fit for union with Brahma. Thus the various sacraments were meant to remove the sin from the body and to purify it. The āryas or the twice-born distinguished themselves sharply from a Shūdra, not so much on racial grounds, but on the grounds of purity, which was largely due to sacraments done for generations.

A question may be asked, What is the purpose of going into details regarding the ideas of the writer concerning purity and pollution when we are considering the question of castes? The answer is a very simple one. I have pointed out elsewhere that the chief principle on which the entire system depends is that of purity and pollution. The Brāhmana is at the top of society be-

the purity to a Brāhmana. The purity of Brāhmana's blood is acquired by generations of pure conduct, which consists of doing actions that are pure, eating pure food, by increasing his own personal sacredness, by the study of Vedas, and by marriage only with people who have kept pure conduct. Their abstaining from marriage with other castes does not come so much from their pride of birth, but is due more to their pride of purity, which would be contaminated by less sacred connections. How far other Hindu castes have a corresponding feeling I am unable to say. But I would not be surprised to find any such feeling amongst the other high castes toward the lower castes, and against the foreigners.

cause he is more pure and sacred than other castes, while Mahar and Paraiyan are at the bottom because they are impure. Thus purity is the pivot on which the entire system turns. Rank, social position, economic condition have no direct effect on the gradation from the standpoint of caste. They are simply aids to establish the status. Caste in India is strong and rigid because the ideas of the people regarding purity and pollution are rigid.[7]

We find in our text that various articles, hours, conditions, and places, almost everything that can be imagined, were graded according to their supposed purity and impurity. The status of a caste or a tribe always depended on the karma,[8] which in various degrees might be pure or impure. The wide range and the minute gradation of substances and actions with regard to purity and

[7] Gautama is very often barbarously complimented as a man who fought against caste, and his creed is very often called a revolt against caste system. The disproof of this matter is needless here, but I may take the liberty of reminding advocates of this creed that the pretensions of the Buddhists regarding purity and pollution were at least as extravagant as those of the Brāhmana, and Gautama is not free from the guilt of promoting such pretensions. In cases he has shown much greater stupidity in these matters than that of all Brāhmanas put together.

Mr. Rhys Davids has shown the fallacy of complimenting Buddha for breaking caste in his various introductions to the Dialogues of Buddha. Robert Chalmers also exposed the attitude of Buddhism toward caste in his article "Madhura Sutta on Caste." (J.R.A.S., April, 1894, pages 360–366.)

[8] The word "karma" was used in various senses. In philosophy it was used as a term expressive of the idea of "motion" as Spencer has used it. Here karma was supposed to operate on matter to produce various things. It was also used to denote that action by animate objects which governed their fate. In popular usage it was also used to denote occupations and other various actions. When applied to the topic of caste it was indiscriminately used in its philosophical as well as popular senses.

pollution is the condition which made the gradation of castes a possibility. To sum up, in short, the caste system sought its justification in the theories of karma and transmigration of souls. The various gradations were simply a natural result of wild and monstrous ideas regarding purity and pollution. The chief objection to the fusion of var*n*as was that it would lead to the discontinuance of oblations. This discontinuance would lead the forefathers to hell and would cause the destruction of everything.

CHAPTER VII.

DISCRIMINATION ON ACCOUNT OF VARNA.

1. *Materials for Investigation.*

Now we come to a subject-matter more important—the treatment of different castes by civil and criminal law and discrimination for the reason of var*n*a. Here the reader should note the fact that there was no discrimination advised by dharma writers on the lines of jāti, but they only advised that some discrimination should be made between the var*n*as. Here the differences in the ceremonial and the discriminations at the court against some var*n*as deserve our attention. We should try to find out if any of the var*n*as were endowed with any peculiar privileges, political or social.

While narrating what our text has to say on these different points, the consideration of its value becomes imperative. I have already said that our text is a book on dharma, whose primary object is to tell, not how things actually were, but how things ought to have been. Thus the text throws on us the task of determining how the things were. The injunctions of the texts are by no means facts. A dharma writer may give a certain precept, but it is our duty to find out the likelihood of that precept being followed.

A peculiar situation under which dharma writers wrote their texts should be noticed. The kings were the persons who were supposed to maintain the privileges of different var*n*as, on the recommendation of dharma writers.[1] If the king did not care to maintain the privileges there was nothing to prevent him except the fear of hostility of the powerful classes. Under these conditions the dharma writers would exaggerate the claims, being sure that only part of them would be fulfilled. If detailed rules are given about anything, the principles at least would be considered by the king. The motive of the author was to create a feeling, mainly among the Brāhmaṇas, which would lead them to guard jealously their own interests. From the standpoint of equity these Brāhmaṇa dharma writers have shown themselves worse than they really were. For these reasons, if there be any part which deserves our greatest suspicion regarding its validity it is the exposition of the privileges and disabilities of various varṇas in the civil law, and of discriminations in the criminal law and especially that portion of the civil and criminal law where the author may be loud regarding the privileges of a Brāhmaṇa. Unless what our writer says is corroborated by other evidence we cannot be sure that the social privileges and disabilities of various varṇas were actually maintained as our text recommends.

First of all let us take stock of all the material at our disposal which may yield us some evidence to form an opinion as to whether the conditions were actually such

[1] In ancient India, the judge with the help of the assessors investigated the case, and informed the king of their result, and the king gave the punishment. Such was the procedure followed in the drama of "Toy-Cart" (Mṛichchakaṭika) where Charudatta is tried. The judge informed the king that Charudatta was guilty of murder, but he being a Brāhmaṇa is not, in accordance with Manu's injunction, fit to be killed. And in this special case the king refused to show mercy to Charudatta and sentenced him to death.

as our writer would have had. The literature of the third century — where I have placed our author — is not well determined. Of the dramas, poems, and Purāṇas none is placed in the third century definitely as far as I know. It is possible that some interpolations in Purāṇas and in two epics belong to this date, but as yet they are not carefully singled out.

Purāṇas as well as the two epics would form very doubtful material for facts, as far as the privileges of different varṇas are concerned. The motives of the compilers of both classes of literature were nearly the same. Authors of one would support a thesis by a Vedic text, while those of the other would maintain it by a tale. For these reasons the Purāṇas in the present condition of research are of little value to us.

However different is the case of literary productions like dramas and poems, yet this source of information has one serious flaw — the distance of centuries from our document. Almost all the dramas that are known to us have been placed somewhere between the sixth and the eighth centuries. These dramas to a certain extent represent the life of the people of the period.[2] But while

[2] Here I feel bound to make some digression to bring to the notice of the reader, that we should accept with great caution the manners and customs as they are reflected in the dramas, as real manners and real customs. We should not take these customs and manners too seriously, for they may be as imaginary as the plot. As a matter of fact only a few dramas in the various Indian literatures reflect the actual conditions of society. First of all it is customary among poets to describe manners that are more charming than true. There is a possibility that some manners may become standard among dramatists and later dramatists may find it difficult to divorce themselves from such a tradition. I have noticed in Bengali literature, many novels and plays full of supposed Rajput man-

interpreting the manners and customs of society, the elements that are likely to be imaginary should be carefully searched out and expunged.

For the verification of dharma injunctions, poems like Raghuvansha also are of very little use. When poets idealize their princes they are sure to describe the lives of these princes as closely in keeping with the rules of dharma and other sciences.[3] But dramas like the Toy-

ners instead of Bengali manners. In some works men and women are depicted as discussing learnedly, and making love, as one may find in European society, while the fact that Bengali women are ignorant and Purda-ridden is well known. Though since 1890 Maratha novelists and playwriters are taking a greater amount of pains to represent facts as they are, still I have noticed in one or two very recent popular dramas, imaginary names and even imaginary geography. Almost every playwriter feels uncomfortable if he cannot introduce a love scene in his play, though there is no such thing as making love before marriage in Maratha society. Even in introducing names they often resort to names that are more high sounding than true and actually found in society (the puritanic and orthodox spirit of Marathas prevent having even high sounding names for their sons and daughters, though they like such names in the plays). Gujarathi and Hindi novels have the same tale to relate. When we try to interpret dramas for historical purposes, we should always guard against the possibility of survival in literature of conditions and manners that are long dead and gone, and against wilful depicting of imaginary manners. The love scenes that are depicted in Kalidasa's Shākuntala, and Vikramorvashiya are by no means a picture of his times; I am also inclined to doubt the reality of the love scenes even in the works like Dashakumāracharita.

[3] With the aid of the commentary of Mallinātha, I have found various passages in the first three cantos of Raghuvansha, which imply some similiarity of the lives of the princes with the precepts of dharma and nīti, and even with the rules of astrology regarding conditions on which good luck depends. The passages which can be compared with Mānusm*r*iti are canto i, 58, 62, 76, 85; canto iii, 11, 33. Those having such relations with other dharma writers are canto i, 8, 20, 25, 76; canto iii, 28, 31, 38, 39. The statements from Raghu which can be compared with the advice of Da*nd*anīti literature are i, 26, 59, 63; iii, 30. But this relation is of very little use to us excepting to show that the poet and his commentator admired that prince best who followed dharma and nīti.

cart (M*r*ichchakat*i*ka) which are realistic in their tone are of greater value to us. If we eliminate the love affairs in these tales, Dashakumāracharita also is of value in explaining the customs of the times.

Another way to determine how far the injunctions of dharma were likely to be followed is to find out how far they were indorsed by the science called nīti. Nīti was a science of moral precepts like dharma science, but the great difference between dharma and nīti was that dharma's authority was due to the fact that it was based on Vedic literature, while nīti derived its authority from its innate worth.[4] Nīti stands in the same relation with dharma as the wisdom literature stood with the propheti-cal and the legal literature (revealed and ritualistic) amongst the ancient Hebrews.

The sciences nīti and dharma were not supposed to oppose each other but were only complementary. In fact there is a good deal in common between dharma and nīti. Their relation may be graphically represented by two circles cutting each other half way. Nīti was less imperative in its tone than dharma.[5]

[4] In the later Sanskrit literature, and the various vernacular literatures, dharma has received the meaning "Religion," and nīti that of "Morality," but a sharp distinction of this kind was not made in the times we are speaking of.

[5] There was a sort of academic distinction between dharma and nīti. The writers on nīti speak of four faculties (Vidyā) of learning: Trayī, Anvikshikī, Vārtā, and Da*n*da-nīti. Of these, Trayī, which meant Vedic lore, was specially recommended to Brāhma*n*a; Vārtā, science of profit and loss, agriculture, and cattle, was specially recommended for Vaishya; and Da*n*da-nīti (nīti for the ruler), was intended for the king. Dharma-shastras formed a division of Trayī, and the bulk of nīti was put in the books on Da*n*da-nīti.

There was another attempt at classification of sciences and adjustment of the relations of dharma and nīti. Sciences were

The writers on nīti were always men engaged in practical affairs of the state, and very often Brāhmaṇas. It is possible that there may be some Buddhistic writers on nīti, but as yet no such work has been discovered, though I suspect that some interpolations in Shukranīti might have been inserted by them. These Brahmanical writers always supported dharma and advised the king to see that dharma is adhered to. Even dharma advised the king to show respect to the precepts of nīti. But at the same time nīti writers must have been a great check on the extravagant claims of dharma.[6]

Thus if we find any doctrine upheld both by dharma and nīti we have a reason to think that the doctrine is more likely to be followed. But if a writer on nīti does not approve of it, either by flat contradiction or silence, we have reason to doubt whether that doctrine was actually adhered to.

We have inscriptions of dates posterior to the date of the author, which material ought not be neglected in a history of caste These inscriptions give us very little, but whatever little they give has its value. Again, almost all inscriptions are dated, and this fact makes the

classified, according to the principle of objects they served. The objects of man in life were, 1. Dharma (to fulfil the duty); 2. Artha (to gain advantage); 3. Kama (to seek fulfilment of desire), and 4. Moksha (gaining heaven). In this classification nīti was supposed to form part of Artha sciences.

6 It should not be wondered at if we find persons and kings following nīti writers in preference to those of dharma. An ordinary Hindu did not care to act according to dharma, but cared only to act according to sciences (Shāstras). It was by acting according to Shastras that he was to live the best life in this world and the next, and not merely by acting according to Dharma.

evidence gleaned from them of considerably greater importance.[7]

There is another factor which we should consider in examining the truth of any of the statements. If any rule given by our text is also given by writers before him like Vashishtha, Baudhāyana, Guatama and reasserted even by later writers and works like Yajñavalkya, Vishnusmriti, Parāshara, Narada and Brihaspati, then the rule is more likely to be respected.

The Chinese travelers also supply something which is reliable, but it is very little. The Arabic traveler Alberūnī, who traveled in the land during the eleventh century, gives us something on the subject.

It is true that all these sources, the literary data, the nīti writers, foreign travelers, and the inscriptions, belong to dates considerably different from that of our author; but they have one thing in common — the priority to Mohammedan conquest, a matter of considerable importance to the history of civilization in India.

2. *Religious and Ceremonial Discriminations.*

Let us first pay attention to the rules relating to religion and ceremonial, where the varna of men is made by the writer a matter of discrimination.

First of all, the first three varnas were sharply distinguished from the last by the fact that the first three had a right to sacraments with Vedic texts, and consequently had a right to be called twice-born. The Shūdra had no such rights.

[7] Here I confess that my examination of inscriptions to find material to corroborate or nullify the injunction of dharma is restricted to *Corpus Inscri. Indi.* vol. iii.

But it should not be supposed that the rules regarding the sacraments of all twice-born varnas were the same. The method in which persons of different varnas received sacraments differed greatly, according to their varna. Our text gives manifold directions regarding sacraments. It tells what kind of name should be given to a child, what the first and second half of the name should mean, what the proper age for initiation should be, how early the initiation may be performed, and how long it may be postponed. It also gives detailed rules of what color the garment of the student should be, of what material the upper and the lower garments should be made, of what grass the girdle around the waist should be made, of what material the sacred string (Yajñopavīta) should be, of what wood the student (Brāhmachārin) should make his staff, of what height the staff should be, and what formula should be used for begging. I do not care to give the detailed injunctions regarding the different varnas in these matters; I only say that the rules differed in each and every matter, as above enumerated, according to the *varna* (ii, 31–49).

But the difference in the ceremonial did not end here. For the ceremony of clipping the hair different ages were prescribed for different varnas (ii, 65). Our text refers to a belief that for the sake of purification, the higher the varna the farther should the sacred water reach when sipped; *e. g.*, "a Brāhmana is purified by water that reaches his heart, a Kshatriya by water reaching his throat, a Vaishya by water taken into the mouth, and a Shūdra by water touched with the extremity of his lips" (ii, 62).

There are various other places where a line is drawn between Shūdra and the twice-born; but the ceremonies where the first three varnas differed are mainly those enumerated above.

The rules referred to above appear to be of considerable antiquity,[8] and most probably they were followed. The proper observance and the maintenance of the rules rested with Brāhmanas themselves, and this is one of the strong reasons for its proper maintenance. Even to-day there is not much departure from these injunctions, though often disputes arise regarding the eligibility of certain peoples to be called Kshatriya or Vaishya.[9]

3. *Treatment of Different Varnas at Court.*

Let us turn our attention to the rules of our text regarding the treatment of different varnas at the court. It prescribed different formalities for different varnas.

[8] See Ashv. Grihya Sutra, 1, 16; 17, 1; 18; Pāraskara, i, 17, 5; 19, 1–6; ii, 1. Apastamba, i, 1, 5, 8–32; i, 2, 33–43 also given by Baudhāyana and Vashishtha. The rule regarding the naming of the child does not appear to be very ancient. It is repeated only in Vishnusmriti (xxvii, 6–9) which is a very late work but cannot be traced in any of the early texts. The proper observance of the rule presumes a condition of society where the Brāhmanas are numerous enough to be consulted. The negligence of the observance of the rule is not associated with penance of any kind and therefore the chances of the rule being observed become much less. It is also vain to suppose that a Shūdra would have the first part of the name of the child mean something contemptible even if he be a contemptible Shūdra. Again, our text prescribes that the last part of Shūdra's name should mean service, and this rule itself prevents the first one being followed. It is not impossible that Shūdras would have names like Dwija-dāsa.

[9] In Uttararāmacharita, act iv, the guests at the hermitage of Valmīki discovered that Kumāra Lava was a son of Kshatriya from his signs, which an initiated boy of Kshatriya varna bears. Notice also in Raghuvamsha three verses regarding the bringing up of Raghu.

" 'Speak,' thus let him (the judge) ask a Brāhmana. 'Speak the truth,' thus let him address a Kshatriya. A Vaishya should be admonished by (mentioning) his kine, grain, and gold. A Shūdra by threatening him with the guilt of every crime."

" Saying whatever places of torments are assigned by the sages to the slayer of Brāhmana, to the murderer of women and children, to him who betrayed a friend, and to an ungrateful man, those shall be thy portion if thou speakest falsely" (viii, 88 ff).

Our author does not stop here. He devotes twelve more verses in order to advise Shūdra of his responsibility as a witness, and to picture the graveness of the variety of sins that would fall upon his head in case he spoke a lie. By the way, I may say here that our writer or the dharma writers in general did not make this provision to insult the Shūdra purposely. Shūdras in general were ignorant people and did not understand their responsibility as witnesses as well as the more lettered classes did. The formality of asking the witness to swear is intended to make him more serious on the occasion. It is a common experience that the more educated classes need less formality than the ignorant ones.

Our text also provides: "Let the judge cause a Brāhmana to swear by his veracity, a Kshatriya by his chariot or the animal he rides on or by his weapon, a Vaishya by his kine, grain, and gold, and a Shūdra by (imprecating on) his head the guilt of all grievous sins" (viii, 113).[10]

[10] Shukranīti, which treats the procedure of the court, is silent on both the points mentioned above.

Again, in the law of evidence, our writer prescribes: "Women should give evidence for women, twice-born men for the twice-born of the same kind, virtuous Shūdras for Shūdras, and men of the lowest caste for the lowest." He permits that on failure of a qualified witness evidence may be given by women and others. But here he warns that such evidence should be accepted with great consideration. In cases of violence, theft, adultery, and defamation the (eligibility of) witness should not be examined too strictly (viii, 68 ff). He admits the eligibility of all varṇas as witnesses. He says truthful speakers from all varṇas ought to be made witnesses (viii, 63), but in the next following verses exempts some persons from the duty of giving evidence and also denies the eligibility of giving evidence to some. But he mixes together people belonging to both the classes. He says: "The king cannot be made a witness, nor a workman (like a cook), nor dancers, nor Shrotriya, nor a student of Vedas, nor one (an ascetic) who has shaken off connection with the world."

"Nor one wholly dependent, nor one of bad fame, nor a Dasyu, nor one who follows forbidden occupations" (viii, 63 ff).

Regarding the appointment of the officers of justice our text lays down the rule, "But if the king does not personally investigate the suits let him appoint a learned Brāhmaṇa to try them" (viii, 9).

It also recommends that the assessors should be Brāhmaṇas (viii, 11). Moreover, it says: "A Brāhmaṇa who subsists only by the name of his jāti, or one who merely calls himself a Brāhmaṇa (though his origin be uncertain) may at the king's pleasure interpret the dharma to him, but never a Shūdra. The kingdom where the monarch looks on while a Shūdra settles the law will sink like a cow in a morass" (viii, 20, 21).

It is here that we have great reason to doubt as to whether this rule was actually observed. The writers on nīti do not appear to be completely in sympathy with these ideas.

Shukra-nīti says: "If a king cannot decide, he should appoint a Brāhmana learned in Vedas, of good family, self-controlled, impartial, pleasing, firm, afraid of the next world, calm, and acting according to dharma. If a learned Brāhmana could not be obtained, then a Kshatriya should be appointed or a Vaishya who knows the dharma science, but the Shūdra should be avoided with care."

"A king should always appoint one born of the same varna as the king himself, for generally the people of the same varna have the necessary qualities" (iv, sec. 5, 12–15).

Thus we find that both dharma and nīti writers agree in recommending a Brāhmana. Our writer is silent regarding the eligibility of Kshatriya and Vaishya. The work on nīti makes a very strong remark in favor of a Kshatriya. It is not vehement in condemning eligibility of Shūdras for the office of judge. Evidently a Brāhmana judge was preferred, but not greatly. Kshatriyas and Vaishyas also acted as judges. The strong language which our writer has used condemning the appointment of Shūdras suggests that he might personally have known of cases in which even Shūdras acted as judges.

Our writer advises that the assessors also should be Brahmanas. Shukra-nīti indorses this opinion. It says:

"A king who wishes to examine the cases should enter the assembly with learned Brāhmana assessors (iv, sec. 5, 43).

We have in Mrichchakatika a scene of trial (Act ix), where the judge is assisted by Shreshthīs. The word "Shreshthīs" implies that the assessors were chiefs of guilds, and they are again represented as men speaking vernacular which implies that they were not Brāhmanas. The case in the Toy-Cart (Mrichchakatika) may simply be local or belonging to a period different than that of our writer, but it may at the same time suggest that the claims of Brāhmanas revealed by Mānava-dharma-shāstra were not always admitted.[11]

4. *Economic Privileges and Disabilities.*

Let us now consider the economic privileges and disabilities of different varnas as our text implies.

Let us first consider the occupational privileges. The occupations open to Brāhmana were various. He could become a priest, an occupation which was considered proper for his caste, or he could become a soldier, an officer of the state, a money-lender, or even a farmer. But he was not to become a domestic servant. The upper castes always had the privilege of following the

[11] H. H. Wilson in his edition of Mrichchakatika has said that the king might be a Buddhist who did not care to pay any attention to Brahmanical claims and for this reason Brāhmanas may have plotted against him. But this inference does not seem to be warranted by facts. Shakāra, who was brother-in-law of the king, has said that he bends his head to gods and Brāhmana alone. Again, the whole city was more or less Buddhistic, as they did not bear even an animal being killed (Shakāra in Act viii). A plot by a few Brahmins against a Buddhist king would not have succeeded. In order to defy the claims of the Brāhmanas the king need not necessarily be a Buddhist.

occupation of their inferiors but not of their superiors. Shūdra was allowed a considerable margin of occupations. All the trades, like carpenter, physician, barber, elephant trainers, and probably those of goldsmith, etc., were allowed to a Shūdra, but he was supposed to show preference to service in the house of Brāhmaṇa. Unless there were any restraints imposed by the trade guilds this varṇa appears to have a considerable margin of the choice of occupations. And if different occupations were becoming a monopoly they certainly were not becoming so through an injunction of dharma. Dharma writers put restrictions on only one occupation — priesthood. And they left the other occupations almost entirely free. Even the lower castes were not prevented from following occupations of Kshatriya. For any person or tribe which might be strong enough to exact obedience, will make himself or themselves Kshatriya. Success in war did not depend on the mercy of the Brāhmaṇas or of the dharma writers. A man who is strong enough to rule will rule, whether Brahmins call him Kshatriya or not. It is possible that the low castes were not entirely kept off from a king's army. Kirātas and Shabaras were freely employed for fighting when necessary.[12]

[12] It should also be noticed that in Mrichchakatika, Chandanaka and Vīraka, who were officers of the army or police of King Pālaka, call each others barbers, leather workers.

Chandanaka — (making a sign to Vīraka saying that he was a barber) you were wont to carry a dead jackal in your hands, to replace dislocated joints, to flourish a pair of shears, and you are now a general — a pretty general. . . .

Vīraka,—(making a sign, reminds Chandanaka that the latter is a tanner by caste) No doubt (your caste is) vastly pure, when your mother was a tabor, your father a kettle-drum, and your brother a tambourine, but you — you are a general.

Regarding the law about inheritance our text advises: "If there be four wives of a Brāhma*n*a in the direct order of var*n*as, the rule for the division of estate among the sons born of them is as follows: . . . Let the son of the Brāhma*n*ī wife take three shares, the sons of Kshatriya two, the son of the Vaishya a share and a half, and the son of the Shūdra may take one share. . . . Or the Brāhma*n*a son shall take four shares, the son of the Kshatriya wife three, the son of Vaishya shall have two parts, the son of Shūdra may take one share. Whether a Brāhma*n*a have sons or have no sons (by wives of the twice-born castes) he should, according to law, give to the son of a Shūdra no more than a tenth part of his estate[13] (ix, 149-155).

Our writer does not give any rules regarding the division of property of a Kshatriya and Vaishya among sons by wives of different grades.

A Shūdra could marry a wife of his var*n*a only. But he could have slaves and sons from them. Our writer has held that these sons deserve some share in the inheritance (ix, 179).

Our writer gives another very peculiar rule: "Whatever property may have been given by her father to a wife, the daughter of a Brāhma*n*ī wife or her issue shall take that property" (ix, 198), *i. e.*: If a Brāhma*n*a has wives of Brāhma*n*a and Kshatriya var*n*as the daughter of the Brāhma*n*ī should succeed to the property of the Kshatriya woman.

[13] Evidently our writer has contradicted himself. According to the first rule given above the son of Shūdra wife could claim two-thirteenths of the property.

Now let us see how far the evidence of our text regarding inheritance can be corroborated from other sources. Nīti literature and the literary works which I have examined are silent on this point. I could not find any references to substantiate or to nullify the statements made here. There is not much on this subject in the inscriptions which I have read so far. But in the dharma literature there is a good deal on this subject.[14]

The regulations which provide for the division of property among the children from the wives of different castes appear to be quite old. Older works like those of Gautama, Vashish*th*a, Baudhāyana, make provision very similar to those of our text, but with very slight variation.[15] Even later Sm*r*itis, like Yajñavalkya and Vish*n*u, also affirm the same rules. The principle involved in these rules is in accordance with human nature and can be traced almost everywhere in the world where similar conditions have arisen; and I think we can safely say that the rules given by our text in this matter were generally observed in his times.

But very different is the case of the rule given by our writer regarding the succession of the daughter of a Brāhma*n*ī (woman) to the property of her stepmother of different caste (ix, 198). This peculiar rule cannot

[14] In connection with this verse, Dr. Hopkins writes to me that we should take this verse to cover the case where a woman dies without issue, and that dying without issue may be supplied from the preceding verse. There is one objection to such construction that the verse ix, 198, occurs in Mahabharata without ix, 197.

[15] Gaut. xxviii, 35-39; Vasi. xvii, 48-50; Baudha. ii, 3, 10; Vish*n*u, xviii, 1-33, 38-40; Yaj. ii, 125.

be traced in any of the earlier or later writers on dharma. The only place where a parallel passage occurs is in Mahābhārata (xiii, 47, 24, 6). All that we can say regarding this rule is that it represents the claim of the Brāhmaṇas of the period, in the matter of inheritance. Whether this rule was actually maintained by the rulers or not is a matter which needs more evidence before we come to any decision.

Our text also provides that on the failure of all heirs the property of the deceased may be taken by the king. But if the deceased be a Brāhmaṇa the king should not take his property, but it should be distributed among Brāhmaṇas.

Like different rules which I mention this rule also appears to be quite old, and can be traced in some later writers.[16] Though I do not have any evidence from literature other than dharma, to corroborate the rule, I think the very persistence of the claim made by Brāhmaṇa writers on dharma might have had some effect in rendering it sacred and inviolate.

We shall now turn our attention to another very peculiar claim of the Brahmaṇas represented in the following verses:

"From the man who shall truly say with respect to treasure-trove 'This belongs to me,' the king may take one-sixth or one-twelfth part.

"When a learned Brāhmaṇa has found treasure deposited in former times he may take even the whole of it, for he is master of everything. When the king finds

[16] Apas. ii, 14, 5; Gaut. xxviii, 42; Vasishṭha, xvii. 83; Baudh. i, 13, 15–16.

treasure of old concealed in the ground, let him give one-half to Brāhmaṇas and place the other half in his treasury.

"The king obtains one-half of ancient hoards, and metals (found) in the ground by reason of his giving protection and because he is lord of the soil" (viii, 35–39).

Here also our means to find out how far this claim of the Brāhmaṇas was accepted are restricted to the dharma literature itself. The older writers, like Gautama and Vashisṭha, make the same statement.[17] The later writer, Yajñavalkya,[18] repeats the same rule, but Vishnu-smṛiti, another late work, gives long, elaborate rules regarding the distribution of treasure-trove among different varṇas.[19] Even though this writer differs considerably from the other writers in the number of details the principle underlying is essentially the same as in the rules found in our text.

There is very little in our text which advises a king to make distinction by castes in the matter of taxation. It advises that a king, even though dying with hunger, must not levy tax on a Shrotriya, and no Shrotriya, residing in his kingdom, should perish from hunger (vii, 133).

Further on it says: "Let the king make the common inhabitants of his realm who live by traffic, pay annually some trifle which is called tax. Mechanics and artisans, as well as Shūdras who subsist by manual

[17] Gautama, x, 43–45; Vasishṭha, iii, 13–14.
[18] Yājñvalkya, ii, 34–35.
[19] Vishṇu-smṛiti, iii, 56–64.

labor, he may cause to work for himself for one day in a month" (vii, 137–8).

The taxes are something which change very often, and it is vain to expect that all the kings would follow the rules given herein. In a case like this if we find a rule from ancient books repeated in new works on dharma, it becomes an evidence against its acceptability for fact. It shows that the writer, while laying down the rule, did not depend on the actual condition but on old books. Such a course was permissible to him, as he was laying down a rule on the question of how the taxes ought to have been. In the verses quoted above there are two points to be considered: (1) exemption of a Shrotriya from taxes and (2) that Shūdras, mechanics and artisans should be compelled to work for one day, in the place of taxes.

Both these statements are made by earlier writers like Gautama (x, 11, 31), Vasishtha (xix, 23), and Apastamba (ii, 26, 10). And it is very likely that our writer derived his statements from some work on dharma, and as these writers were guided by the principle that the more ancient the rule the greater is the authority as regards propriety. But whether the kings held the same attitude toward such practical matters is much to be questioned. Of works on nīti, we have Shukra-nīti which discusses the subject of taxes (Book iv, sec. ii, 105–130). This work is silent on the question of exempting a Brāhmana and expresses the opinion that the king is entitled to two days' labor in a month from artisans and mechanics (121). This work differs from our text in some other places.

5. Varna and Marriage.

Wherever in the world, phenomena resembling caste are found, there is always a tendency toward maintaining a strong barrier shutting the men of the lower group from the women of the higher group. This barrier often consists of laws, public opinion and perverted ethics.[20] Sentiments maintaining such a barrier are clearly expressed in the rules which all writers on dharma, including our text, give, regarding marriage, courtship, illicit intercourse, and outrage on the woman.

Our text generally approves of a marriage with a person of the same var*n*a, but does not entirely forbid a marriage outside the var*n*a, as later writers have done. "A Shūdra woman alone (may be) the wife of a Shūdra. She and one of his own (var*n*a, the wives) of a Vaishya. Those two and one of his own (var*n*a, the wives) of a Kshatriya. Those three and one of his own (var*n*a) wives of a Brāhma*n*a."

"A Shūdra woman is not mentioned even in any ancient story (V*r*ittānta) as the first wife of a Brāhma*n*a or of a Kshatriya, though they lived in great distress."[21]

[20] In India a woman of Brāhma*n*a caste living as a mistress of a man of the same caste would not be so much condemned and ostracised as a woman who marries a Shūdra. In the United States, a white woman who marries a negro would be more severely condemned than a woman who would become a prostitute.

[21] One of the sources of determining dharma was to follow the conduct of persons virtuous and learned in Scriptures. The knowledge of the conduct of the virtuous which existed in the form of stories was a part of the popular lore. Some of these stories have been incorporated in Mahābhārata.

"The twice-born men who in their folly wed wives of the low castes soon degrade their families and their children to the status of Shūdra."

"A Brāhma*n*a who takes a Shūdra wife to his bed will (after death) sink to hell. By begetting a child by her, he loses Brāhma*n*ahood."

"The manes and the gods will not eat the offering of that man who performs rites in honor of the gods, and of manes, and of guests, having a (Shūdra wife) to assist him, and such a man will not go to heaven."

"For him who drinks the moisture of Shūdra woman's lips, or is tainted by her breath, and who begets a son by her, no expiation is prescribed" (iii, 13–19).

He tells us in the rules regarding the shrāddha ceremony that a Brāhma*n*a who marries a Shūdra female should not be invited to a shrāddha (iii, 155).

Marriage between men of lower castes and women of higher castes was positively forbidden. The marriage regarded as the greatest horror was the marriage of a Brāhma*n*a woman to a man of Shūdra var*n*a. Such marriages are condemned severely by calling their progeny equal to the Cha*nd*ālas. Such marriages must have been really rare and the object of the fiction is to prevent them. Neither our writer nor any other law-writer found it necessary to make the children by "marriages against the grains" (marriages of women of higher castes with men of lower castes) a topic in the discussion of inheritance. But it seems probable that men of higher castes might have married women of lower castes, especially Shūdras. Our writer wishes to condemn such practices strongly.

The rules regarding marriages, which made distinctions, with reference to the *varna* of the bride and bridegroom, did not end here. Dharma writers always have taken into account the *varna* distinction when they approved or disapproved forms of marriages. They also tried to draw the line in the ceremonies that were to be performed at the time of marriage. I have told already that they always took into consideration the *varnas* of father and mother of a man or woman when they laid down rules regarding inheritance.

The Scriptures distinguish eight forms of marriages. Out of these eight forms some were approved and some were disapproved. The disapproved form of marriages, like Asura (purchase of the bride) and Paishachya (appropriation of a woman when she is unconscious), were tolerated in Shūdras.[22] The form called Rākshasa consisted of the seizure of the bride. It was approved for a Kshatriya though condemned for Vaishya and Shūdra (iii, 20–40).

When a man married a woman of an inferior *varna*, he took her, by a ceremony different from that which was used when he married a woman of his own *varna*. Our text says:

"The ceremony of joining hands is prescribed for marriages with women of equal *varna*. Know that the following rule applies to weddings with females of different castes."

[22] Only the first four forms of marriage were recommended for a Brāhmana. The Brāhmanas who took a wife by a less approved form were looked down upon. For "The Veda declares, 'The quality of the offspring depends on the quality of the marriage rite'" (Bau. i, 21, 1; Apas. ii, 5, 21, 4.)

"On marrying a man of higher caste a Kshatriya bride must take hold of an arrow (the bridegroom taking hold of the other end of the arrow instead of her hand), a Vaishya bride, of a goad, and a Shūdra female, of the hem of the bridegroom's garment" (iii, 44-5).

Regarding the position of wives of different var*n*as in the family our text advises:

"If twice-born men wed women of their own and of other (lower castes) the seniority, the honor, and the habitation of those wives must be settled according to the order of the var*n*a."

"Among all twice-born men the wife of equal caste, alone, and not a wife of a different caste by any means shall personally attend her husband and assist him in his daily sacred rites" (ix, 85, 86).

From this meagre information it should not be inferred that a free marriage existed between people of the same var*n*a. Our text simply tells us that the writer did not have any objection to one of the Shūdra tribe marrying with another Shūdra tribe. It is just possible that one caste may not marry with another caste though they both may be called Shūdra by the Brāhma*n*as. Even to-day there are hosts of castes which the Brāhma*n*as called Shūdras intermarriage between which will cause the former no unhappiness. There are differences and distinctions between various castes which Brāhma*n*as call Shūdras, but Brāhma*n*as never recognized these differences.

6. *Varna and Illicit Intercourse.*

A strict barrier between var*n*as and castes is sure to result in the stringent rules regarding adultery. Adultery itself was a heinous offense in India since very ancient times. This offense becomes of very great magnitude in a society where pretensions of purity of blood grow very great. Sentiments against adultery are found in various works, ancient and modern, but the sentiment in our text is not so strong as may be found in older works.

Our writer explains why adultery should be considered as a very grievous offense.

"For by adultery is caused a mixture of the var*n*as among men, thence (follows) sin, which cuts up even the roots, and causes destruction of everything" (viii, 353).

The commentators explain the verse as follows: "If a mixture of the var*n*as takes place, the sacrifices cannot be offered properly, because duly qualified sacrificers are wanting. If sacrifices are not duly offered, no rain will fall and everything will perish" (Medh. Gov. Kull. Rāghavānanda).

In order to bring out clearly the distinction made by our writer, as regards adultery between different var*n*as, it is necessary for us first of all to determine the magnitude of the offense committed by a man with a woman of the same var*n*a, as reflected in the punishment, and it is not an easy task. Regarding the punishment for adultery he says: "Men who commit adultery with the wives of others, the king shall cause to be marked by punishments which cause terror and afterward banish" (viii, 352).

But later on he says: "If a wife, proud of the greatness of her relatives or (her own) excellence, violates the duty which she owes to her husband, the king shall cause her to be devoured by dogs in a place frequented by many."

"Let him cause the male offender to be burnt on a red-hot iron bed; they shall put logs under it" (until the sinner is burnt to death (viii, 371-2)).

Now the question before us is how this incongruity is to be construed. To get some light on the question, I have consulted more ancient works on dharma like those of Baudhāyana, Apastamba, Gautama and Vashishtha, but even there one finds the same contradictions. For example, Apastamba says: "He who has had connection with his teacher's wife shall cut off his organs together with his testicles, take them into his joined hands and walk toward the South without stopping, until he falls down dead. Or he may die embracing a heated metal image of a woman" (i, 26, 1–2). But again he says: "He who has had connection with his teacher's wife shall eat every fourth meal-time a little food, bathe at the time of three libations, passing the day standing and the night sitting. After the lapse of three years they throw off their guilt" (i, 26, 101). He has further on described various small or great punishments and penances for adultery with different kinds of women. Baudhāyana shows the same contradiction. To the violater of the Guru's bed he prescribes the same punishment as Apastamba does in i, 26, 1–2 (see Baudh. ii, 1, 13–15), but later on he expresses his opinion that if a person lives as an outcast for three years his guilt is removed (ii, 2, 14). Such contradictions on this matter appear everywhere in the literature. The meaning of all this appears to be that the dharma writers in order to impress the gravity of adultery prescribe one very severe punishment first; then another punishment which is generally a milder one. It is the latter which they really mean to impose. The statement of the severe punishment side by side is intended to make the offender feel that he is really suffering a very mild punishment in proportion to what he really deserves. When a person approaches a Brāhma*n*a to-day in India to seek atonement for some sin it is quite customary among the Brāhma*n*as to tell the man how grave his offense is, in superlative language, and show how serious a punishment he deserves, and to explain to him how by taking various things into consideration the Brāhma*n*a is prescribing only a small penance. When this custom is taken into account those rules would not be very hard to interpret. When two punishments are prescribed, and if one of them is unreasonably severe, we should know it is the milder one that was followed and the mention of the greater punishment had only educative value.[28]

[28] Some writers very often are found in the habit of discovering analogies and regard that what once prevailed among ancient Jews, must have prevailed among the ancient Hindus. In the Jewish Scripture stoning a woman to death is prescribed as a punishment for an unmarried woman who goes astray (Dr. 22, 20-21), and sinaitic law directs that a priest's daughter shall be burned for fornication (lv, 21, 9). Often those engaged in comparative study of institutions seeing words which carry a meaning similar to the Jewish law, have failed to take enough care to discern the real meaning of the Indian document. I do not know how far the punishment of stoning in the Jewish Scripture was one actually in vogue or whether the mention

In order to get the correct idea of the attitude of dharma writers in this matter I must draw attention to some more of their remarks. In order to condemn attempts toward adultery our writer has defined adulterous acts, and includes therein actions like addressing other men's wives in lonely places, offering them presents, romping with them, touching their ornaments and dress, sitting with them, touching them improperly, or allowing women to touch them thus. All such acts done with mutual consent are adulterous acts. And then in the next verse he says that for these adulterous acts a man who is not a Brāhma*n*a ought to suffer death, for the wives of all the four var*n*as must be carefully guarded (viii, 356–9).

Narration of these vagaries would make one thing certain that the punishment for adultery depended more or less on the whim of the king. Dharma allowed him the widest possible margin. The actual punishment for the offense must have been much more moderate.

Now we should find out whether the magnitude of this offense became great or small in proportion to the high or low caste of the man who committed the offense. We find that in the treatment of this question in many cases our text is very vague. It contrasts cases that cannot strictly be compared, *e. g.*: "He who violates an unwilling maiden deserves death at once, but a man

had simply an educative value. We often find very extravagant punishments mentioned in the Scriptures of different peoples, and they cannot be real punishments. In the Scriptures of the Parsis eight hundred stripes are prescribed for involuntary emission of the seed, and the sin of the voluntary emission of the seed was so grave that it could not be atoned at all (Vendidad. Fargand, VIII, v).

who enjoys a willing maiden shall not suffer that punishment if his caste be equal to hers" (viii, 364).

Here there are two elements to be considered in determining the magnitude of the crime —,the status of the woman, and the force used. Our writer has not analyzed them.

He again says: "If a man of lower var*n*a seeks a woman of the higher var*n*a he deserves death. But if her caste be equal to his, then he should pay the father the price of the bride."

"But if a man through insolence forcibly contaminates a maiden, two fingers deserve to be instantly cut off and he shall pay a fine of six hundred pa*n*as."

"A man of equal var*n*a who contaminates a willing maiden shall not suffer this amputation, but shall pay a fine of two hundred pa*n*as in order to deter him from the repetition of the offense" (viii, 366–8).

This carelessness of our writer is a very clear example of indefiniteness in this matter We are not so much concerned with the details of punishment as with the principles. The indistinctness of the rules does not prevent us from knowing those principles. These rules explain to us clearly that the element of caste of the guilty man was considered in deciding cases of fornication and outrage of unmarried girls.

When the limits of var*n*a were crossed the consent of the woman was of very little importance. When a man of low caste has intercourse with a woman of high caste, the matter, whether the intercourse was committed with her consent or against her will, became of very little significance. This spirit can be traced in the rules just mentioned and is plainly illustrated in the following rules:

"A Shūdra who has intercourse with an adulteress of a twice-born varna, married or unmarried, shall be punished in the following manner: If she was unmarried he shall lose the part (offending) and all his property. If she was married he shall lose everything, even his life.

"For intercourse with a Brāhmanī, a Vaishya shall forfeit all his property after imprisonment for a year; a Kshatriya shall be fined one thousand panas, and be shaved with urine."

"If a Vaishya or a Kshatriya has connection with an unmarried Brāhmanī adulteress, let him fine the Vaishya five hundred panas and the Kshatriya one thousand."

"But even these two, if they offend with a married Brāhmanī adulteress, shall be punished like a Shūdra, or be burnt in the fire of dry grass."

"A Brāhmana who carnally approaches a married Brāhmanī adulteress against her will shall be fined one thousand panas, but he shall be made to pay five hundred if he had connection with a willing one."[24]

"If a Vaishya approaches a married Kshatriya adulteress, or a Kshatriya a married Vaishya adulteress, they both deserve the same punishment as in the case of an unmarried Brāhmana adulteress."

"A Brāhmana shall be compelled to pay a fine of one thousand panas if he has intercourse with married (females of) the two (varnas); for offending a (mar-

[24] If she be unmarried he will pay the bride-price as told before.

ried) Shūdra adulteress a fine of one thousand panas shall be inflicted on a Kshatriya or a Vaishya."

"For illicit (intercourse with) an unmarried Kshatriya woman a fine of five hundred panas shall fall on a Vaishya, but (for the same offense) a Kshatriya shall be shaved with urine or pay the same fine."

"A Brāhmana who approaches unmarried females (of) Kshatriya or Vaishya (varnas) or a Shūdra female shall be fined five hundred panas; but for intercourse with a female of the lowest caste (Antyaja) one thousand" (viii, 374–386).

Let us see what all this means to us. In these different rules there are various elements which determine the punishment. First, what is the varna of the woman who is contaminated? In general, the higher the varna of the woman contaminated the greater should be the punishment to the guilty man; the lower the varna of the man, the more severely he is to be treated. The writer considers the element of consent only in case the Brāhmana holds intercourse with a woman of his own varna; he again draws a distinction between fornication and adultery. In these verses he does not consider fornication with a girl of equal varna, but only considers adultery with equal varna, for fornication with equal varna may result in marriage and the offense need not be treated severely. He prescribes a fine of one thousand coins for adultery by Brāhmana with a woman of all varnas, and for that by Kshatriyas and Varishyas with women of all varnas except Brāhmana. For adultery by a Shūdra with a twice-born woman, or by any varna with a Brāhmana woman, is punishable with death. Fornication is treated less severely than adultery, because adultery is more likely to cause a confusion of var*n*as than fornication will. Though adultery is a graver offense than fornication, and rape greater than adultery, he recommends the same punishment for a fornication with a Brāhma*n*a girl by a Kshatriya as he does for rape by a Brāhma*n*a of a married woman (of bad character) of his own var*n*a. For a Brāhma*n*a to commit adultery with an Antyaja (a person of the outcast tribe) woman is in his opinion an offense twice as great as an intercourse with a woman of one of the four varnas.[25]

[25] I have taken the verses viii, 374-385, in a sense different from that of the Sanskrit commentators and the modern critical students. The difference of opinion lies in the translation of the words "*guptā*" and "*aguptā*." These words are translated by the commentators as women "guarded and unguarded by relatives," and their interpretation is adopted by the modern critics. This interpretation, if adopted, would mean that if adultery is committed with a woman not guarded by relatives the offense is smaller, and if she is guarded by the relatives the offense is greater. I hope that by the words "guarded woman" the commentators and the modern critics do not mean a woman "having her relatives with her to guard" when the offense was committed!

We cannot take the words *guptā* or *aguptā* to refer to the question whether the woman is properly secluded or allowed to move freely. It must be admitted that our writer was not a believer in the complete freedom of women as he has emphatically asserted the doctrine that woman does not deserve entire removal of guardianship (v, 148; ix, 2-3), still he was by no means an advocate of the institution of *purda* (segregation of the sexes) which is so strong in the valley of the Ganges (ix, 10-12).

Again, in order to estimate the gravity of the offense, the consideration whether a woman was guarded or unguarded does not appear to be made by any dharma writer. There is an aphorism (sūtra) of Gautama which may give us some reason to think otherwise. While discussing the punishment to a Shūdra who commits adultery with an ārya woman, Gautama says:

The regulations where women are concerned do not end here. Regarding making love, our text prescribes the following rules:

"From a maiden who makes advances to a man of high caste he (the king) shall not take any fine; but her who courts a (man of) low (varna) let him force to live confined in the house."

"A (man of) low (varna) who seeks a maiden (of) the highest (varna) shall suffer death. He who seeks one of equal (varna) shall pay the nuptial fee if her father desires it" (viii, 315–16).

7. *Varna and the Criminal Law.*

Let us now turn our attention to inequalities and discriminations in the criminal law. On this matter our text has a good deal to say.

"With whatever limb a person belonging to an out-

"If a protector he should be executed" (xii, 3). Bühler has taken the aphorism to mean, "if the woman has a protector then the Shūdra offender should be executed." I interpret the aphorism differently, I think that Gautama means that if an ārya woman is confided to the care of a Shūdra and the Shūdra abuses his trust then he should be executed.

I have taken the word *guptā* to mean a married woman and *aguptā* to mean an unmarried woman and have taken the verses viii, 374–385 to mean a discussion on the offenses of fornication and adultery. The word *guptā* is defined as a married woman who indulges in secret amours in Rasamanjari, 24 (See the word *guptā* in Apte's Practical Dictionary).

The words *guptā* and *aguptā* may also with propriety be taken to mean adulteress and prostitute respectively.

I venture a suggestion to explain the corruption of original sense by the commentators, and it may be taken for what it is worth. Most of the commentators wrote their commentaries during the Mohammedan régime, a period during which the *purda* in Northern India became much more strict.

caste tribe strike his superiors, that limb should be cut off. Such is the command of Manu."

"He who raises his hand or a stick shall have his hand cut off; he who in anger kicks with his foot shall have his foot cut off."

"This person of wretched birth if he tries to place himself on the same seat with a man of higher caste, shall be branded on his hip and be banished, or the (king) shall cause his buttock to be gashed."

"If out of arrogance he spits (on a superior) the king shall cause both of his lips to be cut off; if he urinates (on him) the penis should be cut off; if he breaks wind against him, then the anus."

"If he lays hold of the hair of a superior let the king unhesitatingly cut off his hands. Similarly should his hands be cut off if he holds, also, the feet, the beard, the neck or the scrotum" (viii, 279–283).[26]

While interpreting these verses I must again warn the reader that the punishments prescribed here were hardly anything more than threats. They were intended to produce a certain moral effect which society approved of. The punishments given here are quite old. Older works, like those of Apastamba (sec. ii, 27, 141) and Gautama (xii, 1 and 7), and the later smritis of Yajñavalkya and Vishnu, repeat the same thing. All

[26] In translating these verses I am again compelled to dissent from the Sanskrit commentators, and from those who have depended on them. The word Antyaja does not mean a Shūdra. It means castes which are below a Shūdra, like Chandālas. Our writer has sharply distinguished Shūdra from an Antyaja where he prescribes a fine of five hundred coins for fornication with a Shūdra woman and a fine of one thousand coins for such intercourse with an Antyaja woman (viii, 385).

this evidence serves to show that the Brāhma*n*as were asserting the principle again and again, but it by itself is insufficient to convince us that it was actually observed in practice when cases may have been decided. It is plain enough that the persons of low caste who committed offenses against the persons of higher castes must have been severely dealt with, but the punishment could by no means be so severe as these works give. The guilty persons were probably told how grave an offense they had committed and how severely they deserved to be dealt with according to the rules of dharma. The spirit of the law was probably observed but never the letter.

Whatever criticism is made on the rules laid down by our author regarding assault, the same may be made regarding the rules on defamation.

In cases of defamation the higher the var*n*a of the party injured the greater was the offense; and the lower the var*n*a of the offender the greater was the punishment. Our text says:

"A Kshatriya having defamed a Brāhma*n*a, shall be fined one hundred (pa*n*as); a Vaishya, one hundred and fifty or two hundred; a Shūdra shall suffer corporal punishment.

"A Brāhma*n*a shall be fined fifty (pa*n*as) for defaming a Kshatriya; in (the case of defaming) a Vaishya the fine shall be twenty-five (pa*n*as); in (the case of) a Shūdra, twelve."

"For offenses of twice-born men against those of equal var*n*a, (the fine shall be) also twelve."

"A once-born man (Shūdra) who insults a twice-born

man with gross invective shall have his tongue cut out, for he is of low origin."

"If he mentions the names and birth of the twice-born with contumely, an iron nail ten fingers long shall be thrust into his mouth."

"If he arrogantly teaches Brāhma*n*as dharma, the king shall cause hot oil to be poured into his mouth and ears" (viii, 267–272).

Again the text says:

"For a mutual abuse by a Brāhma*n*a and a Kshatriya a fine must be imposed by a discerning king; on the Brāhma*n*a the lowest amercement, but on the Kshatriya the middlemost."

"A Vaishya and a Shūdra must be punished exactly in the same manner according to their respective castes, but the tongue (of the Shūdra) shall not be cut out" (viii, 277–8).

Our writer has repeatedly spoken of the rule that Brāhma*n*a should never be put to death even for the gravest offense. To sentence a Brāhma*n*a to death means a murder of a Brāhma*n*a.

"Tonsure of the head is ordained for a Brāhma*n*a (instead of capital punishment). . . . Let him (the king) never slay a Brāhma*n*a though he have committed all possible crimes. Let him banish such an offender, leaving all his property to him and his body unhurt" (viii, 379–381).

To slay a Brāhma*n*a was not only a grave crime, but it was one of the five great sins, and for it the greatest penance was prescribed.

The fact that to kill a Brāhma*n*a was a very grave

matter is clear enough. The murder of a Brāhmana is associated with great horror in all Sanskrit literature. In order to insure the perpetuity of grants, even great kings always condemned the revocation of the grant by attaching to it the sin of killing a Brāhmana. Even the enemies of Brāhmana (the Buddhists) did not have any scruples in associating the sin of killing a Brāhmana with the violation of their arrangements (Gupta inscri. no. 5, line 10; no. 7, lines 8, 16; no. 16, lines 11–12; no. 55, lines 39–44) in order to insure its safety.

But with all the graveness attached to the murder of Brāhmanas, it is still doubtful how far they were exempted from capital punishment. Nīti literature is silent on this point, and we have several cases which show that such claims were not adhered to. Charudatta, the hero of Toy-Cart, is sentenced to death for the supposed murder of Vasantsenā. But it may be claimed that it was regarded as an improper thing. Nevertheless there are cases where Brāhmanas were sentenced to death for offenses of much less magnitude. Kāmapāla, the seducer of Princess Kāntimati, is represented in Dashakumāracharita as a person twice sentenced to death, once for seducing the princess and another time for plotting against the king. The hero of Chaura-Panchāshika (probably the poet himself) was another man who was sentenced to death for seducing the princess whom he was appointed to teach. All these cases make us suspect that the rule laid down was not strictly adhered to.

In some cases the punishments for crimes were less to Brāhmana than to other varnas. Our text says: "But men of all castes who perform the prescribed penances must not be branded on the forehead by the king but shall be made to pay the highest amercement. For such offenses the middlemost amercement shall be inflicted on a Brāhmana, or he may be banished from the realm, leaving to him his money and chattels (to Brāhmana himself); but (men of) other (varnas) who have unintentionally committed such crimes ought to be deprived of their whole property; if they committed them intentionally they shall be banished" (ix, 240-242).

"It also says: "But a Kshatriya, a Vaishya, and a Shūdra unable to pay a fine shall discharge the debt by labor; a Brāhmana shall pay it in instalments (ix, 229).

Dharma writers are not always lenient toward the higher varnas. In some offenses the higher the varna the greater was the punishment. Our writer says: "In the case of theft the guilt of a Shūdra shall be eightfold, that of a Vaishya sixteenfold, that of a Kshatriya thirty-twofold, that of a Brāhmana sixty-fourfold, or quite a hundredfold, or (even) twice sixty-fourfold, depending on the nature of the offense."

8. Brāhmana and Shūdra.

A correct idea of our work cannot be given, the relations of the castes cannot be made clear, the pretensions of the Brāhmanas cannot be properly represented, unless some of their boastful language is quoted.

"Brāhmana is born to fulfil dharma. Whatever exists in the world is the property of the Brāhmana. On account of the excellence of his origin he is entitled to all. The Brāhmana eats but his own food, wears but his own apparel Other mortals subsist through the benevolence of the Brāhmanas."

"Know that Brāhmana of ten years and a Kshatriya of a hundred years stand to each other in the relation of father and son. Between these two Brāhmana is the father."

"Let not the king, though fallen into the deepest distress, provoke the Brāhmanas to anger, for, when angered, they could destroy him together with his army and vehicles."

"Let a Brāhmana be ignorant or learned, still he is a great deity. To Brāhmana the three worlds and gods[27] owe their existence. Thus though Brāhmanas employ themselves in all mean occupations, they must be honored in every way, for each of them is a great deity."

"Let the king, after rising early in the morning, worship Brāhmanas, who are well versed in the threefold sacred sciences and learned in policy, and follow their advice" (vii, 37).

"Let him honor those Brāhmanas who have returned from their teacher's house after studying the Veda, for that money which is given to a Brāhmana is considered to be the imperishable treasure of the king. Neither thieves nor foes can take it, nor can it be lost. A gift to one who is not a Brāhmana brings an ordinary reward; a gift to one who merely calls himself a Brāhmana brings tenfold regard, and to one who knows Vedas and Angas, a reward without end" (vii, 82–85).

[27] This pretention is not so very bad as it may seem at the first sight. The idea involved herein was that if the Brāhmanas would not perform sacrifices the gods would be defeated and destroyed by the demons.

The kingdom of that king in whose dominions a learned Brāhma*n*a pines with hunger will ere long be afflicted by famine" (vii, 134). "Brāhma*n*a is the root of sacred law. By his origin alone he is a deity even for the gods, and his word is authoritative for men" (xi, 83–85).

A few remarks regarding whether, with all these claims of the Brāhma*n*a, his life was really happy will not be out of place. One great thing which was decidedly in favor of the Brāhma*n*as was that they had a right to take a gift and beg honorably. Other castes could not have done that. The Brāhma*n*as who were engaged in secular occupations must have exerted a great deal of influence and exacted a prestige on account of their caste. Another great thing which helped them maintain a high status was their superior education. Without education any Brāhma*n*a would have been looked down upon by his caste-fellows. It is this high regard for education which raised them above all and maintained them so. There is no evidence to support the belief that they closed the gates of education to those twice-born castes which were not Brāma*n*as. Our text has repeatedly tried to impress on the king and all other āryas the importance of education. But a heresy which took delight in promulgating contempt regarding the Brahmanical education and culture was gaining ground.

The Brāhma*n*as enjoyed high prestige in the land, but they had more restrictions. On account of the peculiar law of purity and pollution their life was extremely circumscribed. A people whose feelings are based on peculiar ideas regarding purity and pollution are more likely to be hurt and pained, especially when rapacious foreigners like Yavanas, Shakas, and Pahlavas were making inroads in the country. They were again an object of envy by peoples below them. Buddhism was trying to pull them down without becoming itself ready to lift the burden which they carried.

As the Brāhmana was above all and godlike, so was Shūdra at the bottom, with the exception of Antyajas who were hardly regarded as members of society. The Shūdra is spoken of in contemptuous manner, but the elements of sympathy are not entirely wanting.

"They (the Brāhmana employers) must allow to him out of their own family property a suitable maintenance, after considering his ability, his industry, and the number of those whom he is bound to support. The remnants of their food should be given to him, as well as their old clothes, the refuse of their grain, and their old household furniture" (x, 124–5).[28]

Shūdra is contrasted with Brāhmana in several places in the book. In discussing the eligibility for office of a judge, Brāhmana and Shūdra are contrasted. This man without sacraments is not a fit person even to carry the dead of the Brāhmanas. Our text also advises a king that he should select a place to build his capitol which does not abound in Shūdras; and he advises a

[28] The Shūdra is sometimes spoken of as if he were like the modern pariah, but this is a false view. The slave Shūdra was a house-slave and must have come into constant contact with his master. Personal service was his special duty. He lived of course in the Oriental style in his own house (not in the one of his master) but he cooked for his master, etc., and was recognized as a member of society, not an outcast.

Snātaka not to dwell in a place full of Shūdras. He again says that a Brāhma*n*a may appropriate the property of a Shūdra with force. In many of the cases I think he does not mean by Shūdra a person who was serving the upper castes, but people of good position who are uninitiated. The large number of Kshatriya tribes which were coming to be regarded as Shūdras, and the sharp contrast often made between Brāhma*n*a and a Shūdra in various places makes me think that at this period the real Kshatriyas were very few. This period of our text appears to be very near the one in which Kshatriyas and Vaishyas came to be regarded as extinct; and for this condition we have to thank Buddhism.

APPENDIX.

CASTE AND ETHNOLOGY.

In my discussion regarding castes and varnas I have attached very little importance to race. To make my own position regarding the relations of caste and race clear, and to explain my opinion regarding the value of ethnology for the study of caste, it is necessary for me to make at first a few remarks on ethnology itself.

Radical defects of ethnology.—I do not by any means depreciate the value of ethnology. To a student of entire humanity, living and dead, the study of races is of very great importance. But unfortunately the ethnologists have not made the meaning of the word "race" as yet clear to themselves. Does that word mean the people of to-day who resemble each other in one or more physical peculiarities whatever their parentage may be, or does it mean people who are born of the same stock whatever their present similarities or dissimilarities may be? Passages can be cited from the writings of almost every eminent ethnologist which would serve to show that he has confused these two ideas. There should be no middle course. Adopting such, one would simply multiply blunders and create confusion in the science. If ethnologists are to take into account *de facto* similarities and dissimilarities, studies in linguistics and philology are needless for their purpose. Present members of mankind should be examined and classified regardless of their parentage.

What principle should we adopt in our classification of races? Should we adopt the skin color or hair section or facial or nasal indices, or physiological systems? There is no general agreement on this point. Various classifications have been made on the various principles stated above. Every ethnologist takes one or more of them and rejects the rest, but no one has attempted to lay down a criterion to estimate the value of different principles, to base our preference for one or the other.

Professor Walter F. Willcox of Cornell University gives a course on ethnology in that institution. When I discussed the matter with him he expressed his views on the subject as follows: In biology the species are classified with reference to the relative permanence of different characteristics; the same principle may be applied in ethnology; mankind also should be classified with reference to the degree of permanence of various physical characteristics.

This view has not been expressed by Professor Willcox in any of his articles, still I think this view deserves publication and careful consideration. I have not seen this view expressed in any of the treatises on ethnology, but I regard it as one of vital importance to the science. If it should be adopted by progressive ethnologists (and I think it will be adopted) it would revolutionize the whole science.

If we accept the view of Professor Willcox we must admit that the study of ethnology is yet to begin. No one has to my knowledge carefully investigated the relative permanence of various characteristics like the skin color, the cranium, the nose, or the physiological system. Until such a study is made it is vain to attempt classification on the basis of physical characteristics, excepting on differences great in themselves and generally admitted to be very persistent.

But if we accept the historical import of the word "race" that is, people descended from the same original stock, our researches should take a different direction. In this case what we desire is not the present similarities and dissimilarities, but we want to recover the history of human migrations and formation of races. In tracing this history, all information which measurements of skull, nose, face, height, section of the hair, complexion, language, culture could give would prove a useful data not for classification, but for the history. In short our study of races would be a study of the separations, migrations, isolations, convergances, and intermixtures of the members of mankind.

Whether the word "race" is applied to a group of people with the desired physical characteristics or to the peoples born of the same stock, it is not a matter of very serious consequence. Both the studies are of value, and the question of name is not of much importance. If the words "race" and "ethnology" should be given over to one of the studies there would not be much difficulty in finding new terms for the other.

Races in India.— Now to turn the question of races in India and their relation to caste. Before examining the question, let me point out what I consider as a defect in the study of races already made. Risley has divided India in seven racial zones: 1. Turko-Iranian; 2. Indo-Aryan; 3. Aryo-Dravidiana; 4. Scythio-Dravidian; 5. Dravidian; 6. Mongolo-Dravidian, and, 7. Mongolian. He has described the characteristics of these different ethnic types, and has given their history. Risley has made his observation carefully. I have gone over his observations, and I think that the seven divisions he made are proper. But Risley in his classification has followed two different principles and has tried to reconcile them. He has studied the physical similarities and differences of the people of various provinces, and with the help of those similarities and differences, he has tried to make a surmise regarding the ancestry of various peoples. He has assumed that the various physical characteristics which distinguish different peoples in India to-day are permanent enough to justify our making an inference regarding their ancestry therefrom.

I do not think that our present condition of knowledge regarding the relative permanence of various physical characteristics should warrant us drawing any conclusion regarding the ancestry of the people of to-day. The history of the migrations of castes and tribes is yet to be worked out, the influence of the environments of different parts of India on the physique of the people and the differences caused on the physique by different economic conditions are yet to be studied. Under these conditions I do not think we are justified in making a division of the people on the basis of ancestry.

Some of the speculations of Risley are too bold,

particularly the one regarding the Marathas. He has called the Marathas descendants of the Shakas or the Scythians. I think Risley is mistaken in his surmise. Moreover I do not approve of affiliating a well-known race like the Marathas to a race like the Scythians of which we know very little regarding most essential points for ethnology.

For example: It would not be difficult to settle whether the present Marathas are more closely allied to the Caucasians or Mongolians. On the other hand, whether the Scythians were Caucasians or Mongolians is yet a matter for controversy. The only advantage one can find in using the term "Scythians" is that this word is more known to the Europeans, and is found in the classical works; and to adopt that word would be in conformity with that usage which prefers terms like the Teutonic race and the Latin race. But we should remember that accuracy is of greater importance than uniformity.

The words "Aryan" and "Dravidian" also are very dangerous to use. I would much prefer geographical terms, or terms based on the present races or tribes.

To sum up my view in short, I approve of seven divisions of India which Risley has made, but I do not approve of the names he has given, and I regard his attempt to discover the ancestry of the races as one very imperfect.

My view of the question of races in India is as follows: All the people of India to-day with the probable exception of the Bengalese and the northeastern frontier tribes are peoples of the Caucasian race. I consider the Dravidians as a branch of the Caucasians.

Excepting in the complexion the Dravidians do not differ very much from the Caucasians of Europe. This view of mine is in agreement with that of Sir H. Keane, who, as appears to me, gives more importance to the present characteristics than to ancestry. The physical difference between the recognized descendants of Aryans and the descendants of Dravidians is not any greater than the physical difference between the Jews and the Gentiles of Europe.

I think that the seven divisions of the peoples of India made by Risley are justifiable. But the names cannot be justified. Of the present Indian population what part is descended from the Rig Vedic Aryan immigrants, and what part is descended from those who were already natives of the country at that time is a question not yet properly approached. Again, we are not yet positive that all the people in India at the time of Rig Vedic immigration spoke "Dravidian languages." The settlement of this question demands much more laborious research than has been done at present, and perhaps the question may never be settled.

Relation of caste and race.—If we take the word "race" in its larger sense, I do not believe there is a very great relation between caste and race. It is true that in some parts the higher castes are of Aryan descent and the lower ones are of Dravidian descent but this is not universal. The conquering tribe will be of a higher caste, whether it is an "Aryan" or a "Dravidian" tribe; the conquered tribes also may be of Aryan race, still it would be of low caste, because it is a conquered tribe. The word "var*n*a" need not confound us; it is a relic of conditions long gone by.

INDEX.

Index to the Passages from Mānava Text Referred or Quoted.